Uniform of the Steward

Uniform of the Steward

Dressing Ourselves for a Life of Faithful Service as Partners in God's Creation

PAUL STEPHENSON

RESOURCE *Publications* • Eugene, Oregon

UNIFORM OF THE STEWARD
Dressing Ourselves for a Life of Faithful Service as Partners in God's Creation

Copyright © 2025 Paul Stephenson. All rights reserved. Except for brief quotations in critical publications or reviews, no part of this book may be reproduced in any manner without prior written permission from the publisher. Write: Permissions, Wipf and Stock Publishers, 199 W. 8th Ave., Suite 3, Eugene, OR 97401.

Resource Publications
An Imprint of Wipf and Stock Publishers
199 W. 8th Ave., Suite 3
Eugene, OR 97401

www.wipfandstock.com

PAPERBACK ISBN: 979-8-3852-4506-2
HARDCOVER ISBN: 979-8-3852-4507-9
EBOOK ISBN: 979-8-3852-4508-6

05/02/25

This publication contains the opinions and ideas of its author and is designed to provide useful information in regard to the subject matter covered. It is sold with the understanding that the publisher is not engaged in rendering legal, financial, tax preparation or other professional services. Laws vary from state to state and if the reader requires expert assistance or legal advice, a competent professional should be consulted. Readers should not rely on this (or any other) publication for financial guidance but should do their own homework and make their own decisions. The author and publisher specifically disclaim any responsibility for any liability, loss, or risk, personal or otherwise, which is incurred as a consequence, directly or indirectly, of the use and application of any of the contents of this book.

A word about the Word
Well, more than a word. The scripture quotations contained herein are from the New Revised Standard Version Bible (NRS), copyright © 1989, by the Division of Christian Education of the National Council of Churches of Christ in the U.S.A. Used by permission. All rights reserved. Or scripture taken from the Holy Bible, New International Version © (NIV). Copy write © 1973, 1978, 1984 by International Bible Society. Used by permission of Zondervan. All rights reserved. Or The Living Bible, (TLB) copyright © 1971 by Tyndale House Publishers. All rights reserved. Or The New Jerusalem Bible (NJB), copyright © 1999 by Doubleday, a division of Random House. Inc. and Darton, Longman & Todd, Ltd. All rights reserved. Or The New English Bible © (NEB) 1972. The delegates of the Oxford University Press and the Syndics of the Cambridge University Press 1961, 1970.

Contents

Introduction   vii
Meet the Stewarts   ix

WHAT IS THE UNIFORM OF THE STEWARD?

What is Stewardship?	3
Stewardship	20
Prudence, Prosperity & Knowledge	20
Stewardship Trust	28
Purpose of Money	33
Tithing	40
Putting Stewardship into Action	45

OLD TESTAMENT FOUNDATIONS

Caretakers of this World	55
That's Obey, Not eBay'	61
Disciple, as in Discipline	65
Character	75
God's Promise to the Tither	81

NEW TESTAMENT LESSONS

From Discipleship to Stewardship	87
From Giving as Obedience to Giving as Love	103
Stewardship: A Spirit-Filled Great Commission	118
Epilogue	137
Lord Jesus	138
Bibliography	139

Introduction

BEFORE TIME BEGAN, THERE was only God, watching over a vast and swirling chaos of dust, water, and light. The angels, curious as ever, asked, "What will become of this?"

God smiled and began to gather the dust, shaping it into great spheres. "Some will shine as stars, some will be solid as mountains, and some will simply drift." Then, God took the water and placed it into rivers, lakes, and vast oceans. "Some will nourish the land, some will rise as clouds, and some will simply flow."

The angels looked upon what God had done and said, "This is beautiful! Is it finished?"

God's voice echoed, "Not yet."

From the earth, God brought forth trees that stretched toward the sky, creatures that crawled and soared, and life that pulsed in all its forms. The world filled with motion and song, but still, it was not complete.

Then, God shaped two beings from the dust and water, breathing life into them. "You are stewards of this world. It is nearly finished, but I leave the rest to you."

The man and woman looked around, overwhelmed. "But how can we complete something so vast? We are small, and only You know the way."

God knelt beside them and said, "You do not work alone. I am your partner. A partner is someone who walks with you, shares the burden, and never gives up. There will be days you feel I am silent, and days I may think you are idle, but even then, we remain partners in this work."

The two nodded, accepting the task.

The angels, still watching, whispered, "Is it finished now?"

God looked upon the man and woman and answered, "I do not know. Ask my partners."

And, in 1998, Sarah and Michael Stewart created Thomas, one of God's new partners.

This book is about dressing ourselves for a life of faithful service as one of God's partners or stewards. Imagine a life of faithful service where we prosper spiritually and have financial security. We can have prosperity both spiritually and financially. Some of us will have one or the other. Some of us will have both. One thing is certain, if you have money but not life, you have nothing. Life is not the result of money.

This book is for those who struggle with what stewardship really means in their life. And I am one of you! We need this book.

Most books about stewardship are about money. This one is about becoming faithful with what God has first given to us. Don't worry, it will deal with money. But understanding what the uniform of the steward is will come first. To help us with our understanding, we will drop in on Thomas Stewart and follow his journey of putting on the uniform of faithful service of stewardship.

Let us begin our journey with Thomas by getting to know him a little better. And where better to start than with his parents, Sarah, and Michael.

Meet the Stewarts

SARAH WAS RAISED CATHOLIC. She came from your typical Middle American family; went to Sunday school, had first communion, and went through confirmation. She had good grades in school, not great, just typical. She went to college, got her degree, and fell in love with Michael.

Michael was your characteristic American boy. He played sports, went to church most of the time and just did boy stuff. Michael was Presbyterian and found church okay, not inspirational, or profound, just okay. Like Sarah, Michael went to college, met Sarah there and were just friends until the summer of their senior year. During that summer, they both had the same job on a cruise ship, being ship stewards. That's when they fell in love with each other.

After college, they both got jobs, Sarah being a cruise ship steward. Michael is a hotel steward. They loved their jobs and each other, so decided to get married. A few years after that, Thomas came along.

Now Thomas wasn't raised totally Catholic or totally Presbyterian. Because of his parents' careers, he moved a lot; Miami, Galveston, New York, San Diego, Orlando. Both Sarah and Michael thought church was important and wanted Thomas to have a similar religious upbringing to that they had as kids. But because of their jobs, they just went to the church that was closest to home at the time. So Thomas spent time as a Lutheran, Pentecostal, Methodist, Catholic, and Presbyterian.

Growing up, Thomas, like his parents, was a typical kid. He got average grades, went to church when he could and went to college. As a child he was always fascinated by the cool uniforms his parents had for their jobs, which led him into a career as a tailor, manufacturing commercial uniforms.

Lately, Thom has been worried about his finances. He's doing okay but thinks he could be doing better. He'd like to get married, have kids, and have enough to provide for their future and retirement. He's stressing about how concentrating on trying to become financially secure is affecting his relationship with God. Thom would be considered part of the Christian Middle Class, which are in financial trouble. Financial trouble is the root cause of other troubles: worry, guilt, stress, lack of freedom. It is also a symptom of other root causes: an impaired relationship with God, your spouse, your kids, and yourself.

What got Thom to worrying about was a conversation he had with one of his co-workers last Friday. His co-worker told him this story:

> What the man said, "If I had some extra money, I'd give it to God. But I have just enough to support myself and my family." And the same man said, "If I had some extra time, I'd give it to God. But every minute is taken up with my job, my family, my clubs and what have you every single minute." And the same man said, "If I had talent, I'd give it to God. But I have no lovely voice. I have no special skill. I have never been able to lead a group. I can't think cleverly or quickly the way I would like to." And God was touched. And although it was unlike Him, God gave the man money, time, and glorious talent. And then He waited. God waited and continued to wait. Then after a while God shrugged His shoulders and he took all those things right back from the man-the money, the time, and the glorious talent. After a while, the man sighed and said, If only I had some of that money back, I'd give it to God. If only I had some of the time, I'd give it to God. If I could only rediscover that glorious talent, I'd give it to God. And God said, "Oh, shut up." Then the man told some of his friends, "You know, I'm not sure that I believe in God anymore."

That got Thom to thinking, "Am I like that, is that me, am I turning into that guy?" Which lead to the worries he has now about his future and how God fits into all of it.

That night as he was checking his emails at home, he saw an email from the church he drops into now and then. They sent a blast email of their Sunday announcements. This Sunday's sermon was called: Biblical Stewardship: That Which Is of True Value. That piqued his interest. So he thought he would attend, providing of course, if he didn't sleep in.

Thom did make it to Sunday services and as he prepared to listen to the sermon, the Preacher began, "Biblical stewardship does not require that a Christian despise money or to discontinue earning it." That got his attention. The Pastor went on, "Biblical stewardship requires that Christians view money differently from the way the secular world views it. The secular world equates affluence with success and happiness. Therefore, society constantly struggles to acquire as much wealth as possible. The Bible, however, exposes the worthlessness of such a struggle by revealing the truth about money. The Psalms proclaim, 'But man, despite his riches, does not endure; he is like the beast that perish.' (Psalm 49:12) No matter how much one struggles for wealth, death still awaits because money cannot add anything to one's life.

One could argue that, although money does not keep death away, it is still worth pursuing because it brings happiness and satisfaction in life. Solomon, a wise and rich man, argues, 'whoever loves money never has money enough; whoever loves wealth is never satisfied with his income. This too is meaningless. As goods increase, so do those who consume them. And what benefit are they to the owner except to feast his eyes on them. . .the abundance of a rich man permits him no sleep.' (Ecclesiastes 5:10–12) Money is meaningless. It can never satisfy those who love it and instead offer frivolous goods and anxiety."

Thom thought, did he just say anxiety, as in worry. Yeah, that's just what I'm going through!' Thom began paying even closer attention as the Preacher concluded, "the struggle for wealth brings with it dissatisfaction, not a better life. When money is not the object of one's love and devotion, one is free to focus on higher things. Those last two words, higher things, stirred something deep inside Thom. It triggered a curiosity to know more, to learn more, to be more. As a tailor he knew that quality materials make quality garments. And what he heard was quality material. He wanted to find out what are the quality materials that make up stewardship. And with those quality materials he could craft a pattern that could be sewn together into a uniform, a uniform he could wear. A uniform that had embroidered into it both spiritual and financial prosperity. A uniform that let him be a faithful servant to God. A uniform that let him focus on higher things. A Uniform of the Steward.

Pray

We hold fast to the conviction that we are all responsible for being good stewards of our time, our resources and our compassion in a broken world. Every person has something to give in return for what has been received. Amen.

What Is the Uniform of the Steward?

What is Stewardship?

THUS BEGAN THOM'S JOURNEY to find the quality materials that comprised what stewardship meant to him. Like most of us, he began with what he knew. Which he quickly found out, wasn't that much. He was quite familiar with what a steward was in the secular world. He witnessed it through his parents as he grew up. He knew stewards help others, are courteous, have good customer service skills and typically carry out their duties cheerfully.

Growing up he recalled his parents talking about how the Steward was in charge of the Upper Ten and Lower Five household servants of the old English manor houses. Although there were slight variations from house to house, the domestic hierarchy was an accepted established system which expected certain specialist skills and services from each of its members. Those who rose to the top of the tree were deeply knowledgeable men and women, knowing not only their own work but also what to expect from their underlings, some of whose jobs they themselves had done on their way up. As rigidly as any trade union members today, they accepted that there was a special task for every person and a special person for every task. That always reminded Thom of how the Bible talks about everyone serving God with their own special talents.

He even remembered asking his mom once what the word "steward" meant. Her answer was the steward was the "keeper of the hall" and was the official in a medieval household responsible for its management. He thought medieval sounds cool with knights, dragons, and castles. She continued the lord of the castle had all of the legal authority; the steward had only a delegation of that authority and a mandate to administer the estate. The steward, she said, needed to hold himself accountable for all that took place in the household. Wow, he thought that sounded like a pretty important job. And since both of his parents were stewards, they too must have pretty important jobs. How cool is that? To have parents with important jobs that go clear back to olden, medieval days.

Okay, that was then, it was a nice story Thom's mom told. What about now? As an adult, Thom figured he should start with the basics. So he Googled steward and found a "stigweard" is an Old English term for steward. Stig meaning "house" and weard meaning "warden or keeper." Webster's online dictionary defines a steward as one employed in a large household or estate to manage domestic concerns including supervision of servants, collection of rents and keeping of accounts. Further Google® research showed Thom the office of steward is not only one of great responsibility, but it is also an office that requires great accountability. Stewards have no inherent authority of their own. Their authority is entrusted to them by their master.

Thom had the notion when we acknowledge God as our Master and that we are created for a vertical relationship with God, we come to see ourselves as God sees us: stewards. Stewardship is how we serve God in our role as his stewards. Stewardship is everything we do after we accept Christ.

As Thom began to ponder that, certain truths he held about stewardship became myths bursting. Like, the congregation's stewardship is primarily a matter of paying the church bills, faith and finances don't mix, stewardship is best motivated by guilt and encouraging congregational stewardship is the job of the pastor and council.

Stewardship is not an annual fundraising campaign. It is a lifestyle to which God has called us. True stewardship for the New Testament believer grows from grace. It recognizes that "all are yours and you are of Christ and Christ is of God (1 Cor 3:22–23)." It's not just about giving money. Christian stewardship is really nothing less than all we do with all that we have. In other words, all of the spiritual and natural "money" of God is at our disposal. The bolt of cloth is in our hands. What are we going to make out of it?

Thom also did a biblical word search on stewardship and found over 2500 references. That was curious to him because the subject of stewardship is not frequently mentioned at his church in worship or prayer until there is a severe shortfall of finances. He tried to imagine what stewardship would look like if it were synonymous with spiritual formation. Such stewardship might look like generosity. It might resemble lifelong learning. It could look like discipleship, the discipleship we share as followers of Christ. So he thought stewardship is better described as a compound term like "giving-serving" or "generosity-living."

In Thom's head the image of stewardship as discipleship, this included money but not limited to money, started forming. The first pieces of the pattern for his uniform of the steward were beginning to take shape. You need to be disciplined or have discipleship. And you are put in charge of something that belongs to somebody else. So what is it that I'm in charge of Thom thought? If I'm going to be a good steward, I have to know what I'm in charge of, I have to know what I have, what I'm good at.

If I don't know what my gifts are or what my talent is, then I'm wasting my time. Like my mama use to say, "It's like putting fertilizer on concrete and expecting grass to grow!" I need to assess my situation before I spend a lifetime perfecting imperfection.

This thinking leads Thom to another realization: That it just might be okay to be successful. That if he discovered what he was really good at, like tailoring; God would want him to be successful at it. It would be his responsibility to learn and follow God's vision for his optimal future. That it's just as sinful to live beneath your means as it is to live above them. Poverty doesn't automatically make you more conscious of God or more spiritually minded. Furthermore, God doesn't stop speaking to the rich. He speaks to anybody who has a listening heart, regardless of the balance in their checkbook. He remembered that Jesus refers to the "poor in spirit," not the poor in finances. He is speaking about those who are humble, who have no pretense that they are beyond any need of God's forgiveness. In other words, have an attitude that they need God and are spiritually destitute without him.

Thom recognized that if God wanted him be successful, he had to be ready to handle success successfully. He had to become qualified for success.

Like Noah and Moses, God was calling to Thom. He wasn't sure if he was ready to answer him.

What are you in charge of?

Consider the following questions. Write your answers down, being as specific as possible. Give examples. Give as much space as you need.

1. What unique gifts had God bestowed upon you?
2. Are you using those gifts or denying them?
3. What is the first step you could take to use those gifts toward your future?
4. What would it take for you to realign your life with your gifts as your guide?
5. What do you most enjoy doing? (What are your joys?)
6. What can you do? (What are your competencies?)
7. Do your joys and competencies add value to the lives of others?

Now have a few of your close friends answer these same questions about you. See where there are the similarities and differences.

STEWARDSHIP DEFINED

It had been a long week for Thom. The questions he contemplated from last Sunday's sermon nagged at him all week. It was the weekend now and Thom wanted to get back to continue his pattern making on his uniform of the steward. So far, he knew a steward is someone who has been placed in charge of something that does not belong to him. A steward is a temporary caretaker. That was a good start, and he felt there was something more to it, something more meaningful. In the back of his mind he also knew God was whispering to him about being successful with what God had put him in charge of. Thom wasn't quite ready to answer that whisper. He needed more information. So off to the library he went. He figured he could use the internet there. What he couldn't find surfing the web he could find the old fashion way-in books or ask a librarian.

Like before, Thom began with what he knew. Or, in this case, what he remembered. He remembered going to some confirmation classes as a youth and the pastor talking about a guy named Martin Luther. He recalled Martin believed the pursuit of material well-being through personal industry and trade was to be considered a proper industry and trade was to be considered a proper Christian vocation, just as surely as praying, giving alms, and going to church. That sparked the recollection of the Protestant Reformation from some long-forgotten history class in middle school.

Thom thought, "why not begin with a history lesson and find out what others back in time had to say on the topic."

He discovered John Wesley's theology of stewardship boiled down to "earn all you can, save all you can, give all you can." That William Perkins wrote, "If we happen to have inherited much property, we are to enjoy it in good conscience as a blessing and gift of God." Thom found Wesley's stewardship theology refreshing in light of today's "me" mentality.

The Puritans believed that God was involved in all aspects of life. Those who accumulated wealth could, therefore, explain such prosperity as a sign of their faithfulness to God's calling. If opportunity for profit presented itself to the individual, the conscientious Christian took advantage of the situation. Refusing to do so would indicate an unwillingness to be a good steward and would reflect a desire to turn one's back on God's presence and call.

In the 19th century the concept of God's trustee over everything that he had given you emerged. If you were not a good trustee, then judgment from God would follow. This view developed to combat the view of being a "self-made" person.

From this Thom begins to see another piece of the pattern; that we are managers or partners with God. God has blessed us, wherever we are and whoever we are. All that we have is a gift. Our faithful living and giving are a response to God's love. Since all that we have is a gift, then every part of life is touched by the elemental nature of stewardship.

Thom had the random reflection: learning to be a steward is like growing up. As a child you're not fully aware of all of God's gifts, so you only give a little. As a rebellious teenager you're into taking and not into giving. When you become a wiser adult, you become fully conscious of God's grace and willing to become an obedient disciple. Thom said to himself, "I wonder where I'm at in my growing up."

So far, a few principles of good stewardship have begun to take shape. The who's in charge principle. Where God is owner; we are the managers. The give and grow principle. When you give, God gives back to you. You cannot escape the consequences of one's actions concept. And the identify your spiritual gifts. Know what you're in charge of so you know what to do with it. To be successful at success.

It was lunch time, so Thom took a break from his research and took a stroll around the park next to the library. Reflecting on what he had learned so far, he was thinking to be stewards of the gospel means that we are to continue the work begun by Christ. God uses voices, personalities, money, and possession of human beings to communicate with the world. To shirk the responsibility of being a partner or manager with God means that the kingdom can fall into bad repute. The tragedy for the world and for the church is that the church has often perverted this responsibility to a preoccupation with saving itself. In this light, the activity of God-father, Son and Spirit, is simply to bring us into the joyful relationship of stewardship that God has promised. Stewardship is not manipulation; rather it is an invitation for people to look honestly at God, the world and themselves.

In this light, stewardship is not simply relational; it is communal and global. When we receive the Spirit, we become a steward of God's goodness; but we also enter into a relationship with God's people. Together, as the body of Christ, we are stewards of God's generosity to the whole world.

Thom needed to put the last touches on this piece of the pattern, so back to the library he went.

Browsing the books Thom came across a quote from St. John Chrysostom who said "Not to enable the poor to share in our goods is to steal from them and deprive them of life. The goods we possess are not ours, but theirs." Part of the communal steward relationship is responsible caretaking. As we recognize all things are a gift from God, we subsequently need to share a portion of these gifts with others, especially those in need.

Good stewards or responsible caretakers need to possess three inner qualities: faith, gratitude, and openness of heart. Faith underscores our belief that everything is from above. Gratitude: faith-based people logically will be grateful persons, carrying within their hearts an attitude of thankfulness and expressing that gratefulness publicly as well. A spirit of gratitude deepens our realization that everything comes from God; thus strengthens our faith. Openness of heart: gifts from God, received in faith and with gratitude are not meant to be hoarded or kept for our own exclusively. Instead, we need to share a portion of those blessing from above to others, especially to persons in need. We could categorize those blessing of gifts under the title of time talent and treasure.

Time. In our high pressured, time conscious society, this may be the most challenging gift to share. That sharing can take an unlimited number of forms from volunteering at school or church to staffing a downtown soup kitchen or hospital gift shop.

Talent. This sharing likewise will occur in a countless variety of ways. From mentoring at-risk students to serving on a financial committee for a not-for-profit organization. From using musical talents at church worship to building homes for the homeless in some Central American country.

Treasure. A portion of one's financial resources, ideally a tithe (more to come on that later in the book) goes to church and charity, building up the parish and making this a better world. The latter includes one's personal charities such as caring for an ailing relative, donations to United Way* or support of mission work.

When we receive God's gifts and are willing to share a portion of them with others we seem to flourish and to be full of life. When we cling and do not share, we often appear to stagnate and become lifeless.

Thom sensed he was getting a good foundational definition of what a steward is and wondered how the bible defined it. In his research he kept coming across words like "okimonos" and "oikonomia." It looked all Greek to him, so he sought the assistance of a research librarian to help him decipher these weird words. Funny thing is they really were Greek words. The research librarian told him they were compound words with the roots of oikos, which means dwelling, home, or household; and nomos, which means parceling out, management or administration. So okimonos are translated to mean overseer, administrator, or fiscal agent. Oikonomia is the plural for oikonomos and translates to mean the administration of an estate or household.

So in a biblical sense, a steward (oikonomos) is a person who is in charge of a household or an estate. The administration of this responsibility is stewardship (oikonomia). The steward is not the owner, but he or she has been left in charge of the management (oikonomia) while the owner has gone away. The owner holds the steward responsible for the administration of the estate, just like in Matthew 25:14–30. The steward buys and sells goods, binds, and loses administrative agreements, as we see in Matthew 16:19, 18:18 and John 20:23, always for the benefit of the owner. Thom was pleased to see that his research so far was in-line with what the Bible said about being a steward. There was, however, one other word that Thom wanted to define because it kept popping up as well in his research. That word was disciple.

It was one of those words you always hear but never really put a definition to it. Thom would usually hear it in conversations or sermons. Typically in phrases like, "they were disciples of Christ," or "she's a true believer, a real disciple" or even, "the followers of Jesus, his disciples." Thom thought he had a working definition of the word disciple and wanted to see if it was accurate.

What he found out was the word disciple derives from discipline, as in behavior in accord with rules of conduct; behavior and order maintained by training and control. To be a disciple is to be disciplined to a philosophy, set of principles, or set of values. Disciple to an overriding purpose, to a superordinate goal or a person who represents that goal. In other words, Thom thought, if you are an effective steward, your discipline comes from putting God first; it is a function of submitting your independent will to God's will. You are a disciple, a follower, of God's gospel and you have the will, the integrity to subordinate your feelings, your impulses, and your moods to his Word.

Thomas felt blessed knowing God wanted him to be his partner, his steward. That by following God's word he could discipline himself to become a better steward. Since Thom was looking up word meanings, he quickly looked up the meaning for blessed. He found it means endowed and/or empowered by God. Yes, Thom definitely was feeling empowered, was feeling blessed.

Thom jotted down a quick definition of what he thought stewardship meant:

> Stewardship is the grateful, disciplined response of the whole person continuing the work Christ began. It is dressing ourselves for a life of faithful service as partners in God's creation.

He then held out his hands in front of him with his fists tightly clenched. He slowly opened his left hand to remind him of how you receive a gift. Then he slowly opened his right hand to remind him of how to give a gift. To put on the uniform of the steward you have to have open hands. You can't have clenched fists holding on to what you think your possessions are, thinking to yourself, "mine, mine, mine." You must be willing to have open hands to receive and to give. Then it dawned on him, I shouldn't be going to church out of custom, tradition, or habit. I go because I am a disciple, disciplined to cheerfully follow what God commands.

The library was closing, and Thom wasn't finished yet discovering all the pieces to his pattern for the uniform of the steward. Tomorrow, he thought he would continue his journey by finding out what are God's expectations of his stewards.

Pray

God, help me to be faithful and humble as I steward all you have placed in my trust. Amen.

Expectations of the Steward

When Thom resumed his pursuit the next afternoon, he began by perusing his bible. The first expectation of being a steward he found in the first book, the first chapter. In Genesis 1:28 he found out God created us to be stewards and commands us to be stewards. As he continued to read his bible, Thom saw that God always allows us freedom to make our own choices. We have the option to be faithful or unfaithful. God is too loving and gracious to force us against our will. That as we discipline ourselves to follow his commands, we have a significant role to play as a steward of God's resources. Some of the key expectations Thom found are: we understand that all the world's resources are God's resources (Leviticus 27:30); God has simply loaned us his resources and has the right to expect us to invest them wisely in whatever way he deems appropriate (Matthew 25:14–30); how we spend our earthly riches has eternal consequences (Luke 16:10–12).

Stewardship implies a caretaker role. A good steward manages the resources of the master with the utmost care and concern.

Thom also saw a theme developing from these expectations: financial stewardship. God uses finances to develop our relationship with him. That financial stewardship is something that we are all involved in whether we know it or not.

Thom knew his pattern making would eventually lead him to study this part of being a steward. He figured this is as good as time as any to see how this piece of the pattern would fit into his uniform.

Financial Stewardship

Financial stewardship has to do with the way in which you use your resources to provide for your needs and for the needs of God's kingdom on this earth. Stewardship involves far more that your money. Why? Because your resources involve far more than your money and material goods. Among your resources are your talents, abilities, capabilities, skills, experiences, creative ideas, energy, time, strength, spiritual gifts and much more.

If you want to know what a person believes, just observe the decisions he or she makes. For in the end how you use your resources is simply a magnifying glass for what's in your heart. One of your resources, money, really never gives or takes on its own; it just magnifies what is already in your heart.

> There are over a thousand verses in scripture that deal with financial matters. Over two-thirds of the parables deal with finances and stewardship

---

Thom thought about his own finances and how he deals with money. After all, that's one of the reasons he began this journey. He said to himself, "How does God expect me to handle the money resource"? As he studied the Word and did more investigation, he found God has extremely specific principles in his Word related to money management.

When Thom was reading Cliff Goins' book Stop Digging, he confirmed what he previously discovered: God gave us stewardship over all the resources of the earth. He also realized those resources exist so we can live off the abundance God purposely put in the earth. The earth is one big resource. The way we lay claim to pieces of that resource is with money. The process works like this: We plant and water the resources and God causes the resources to expand exponentially. Now if we decide to consume the resources, then the entire expansion process is cut off-not only for that person but for every person down-line that was depending on that person.

The parable of the talents (Matthew 25:14–30 and Luke 19:12–27) is the story of a man giving his servants stewardship over his goods. In this instance the servants received what they could handle given their ability. What was the result of this stewardship project? The two servants who planted and watered the resources were rewarded with great gain. The one servant who ate or consumed the seed or did not put it to its intended use, did not see any increase and was berated before being cast into the outer darkness for his lack of profitability.

Thom was familiar with the parable, so what is the point the parable is trying to make? The point is that the purpose of money is for us to use money to be profitable in life. What does that mean? When we talk about being profitable, we are talking about being successful. True success only comes from doing what God created you to do. In that success is peace, joy, happiness and wouldn't you know it-money. The most important attitude to embrace about money is this: it is not yours. It belongs to God, and you are supposed to manage it. In order to successfully manage it you have to learn how it works. You have to learn how to be successful at success.

In review

In defining what stewardship meant Thomas discovered:

- The earth does not belong to humanity. It belongs to God.
- Money is merely a universal resource on the earth.
- God uses finances to develop our relationship with him.
- We are managers or partners with God.
- Good stewards or responsible caretakers need to possess three inner qualities: faith, gratitude, and openness of heart.

His working definition of stewardship is:

> Stewardship is the grateful, disciplined response of the whole person continuing the work Christ began. It is dressing ourselves for a life of faithful service as partners in God's creation.

Pray

Lord, as your faithful servant, I pray that I will live a life that is dedicated to you. I long to hear you speak these words at the end of my days," Well done, good and faithful servant." Amen.

PITFALLS THAT LEAD TO SHODDY STEWARDSHIP

God was still whispering to Thom about being successful with what he had put Thom in charge of. And Thom knew that in order to be successful, he had to also know what the pitfalls are. Thom realized that we have all been conditioned by our culture, even our Christian culture, to believe that our contentment is something "out there." he also recognized that a concern about material gain is not in itself ungodly. A concern for material wealth that chokes out and rules over a concern for one's spiritual gain and one's mental, emotional, and family health is ungodly.

We experience life on the inside, not the outside. The kingdom of God is within us. Consequently, outside things do not determine whether or not our cup is full. The dream home, car, or vacation cannot provide any more than a moment of satisfaction. When that moment is over, we are off to the next new thing.

Life is not about things. Our consumer-driven economy is about things. If we believe that life is found in the external things of life as our culture teaches us, we will believe that what we drive tells people who we are.

The Lord desires for us to grow in every area of our lives; to be growing spiritually, physically, mentally, emotionally, in friendships and family ties and in material sustenance. Always in balance and always growing. We are to invest our many abilities, skills, and assets wisely so that growth is possible. When we completely abandon our potential, refusing to do anything with the many gifts God has given us, God is displeased. He is not displeased that we gain wealth. He is displeased when we gain wealth at the expense of all other areas of our lives. God's ultimate goal for our lives here on earth is not comfort, it is character development.

Every moment of every day the deception of wealth leads real men and real women straight into the jaws of hell. Rich or poor, the symptoms of shoddy stewardship are the same: excessive debt, crumbling relationships, growing addictions, living in the future, a sense of hopelessness and of not being in control and a joyless, fruitless life.

Thom found that the pitfalls that lead to shoddy stewardship could be put into three categories: 1. the lust of the flesh 2. the lust of the eyes and 3. the pride of life (1 John 2:15–17). It is our lust, or to use a similar word- desire, which is selfish and draws us away from God. That to be obedient to God to hear, we need to know our own desires and make sure they are toward God. By hearing God (obedient) we may then discipline ourselves (become disciples) for a life of faithful service as partners in God's creation. By aligning our desires with God and obeying his will and not our own will we take away the power of the devil to use our good desires as well as our bad desires.

These pitfalls reminded Thom of how the devil tempted Jesus in the wilderness (Matthew 4:1–11). Where the devil tempted him with his good desires and tried to use those good desires to turn Jesus away from his Father.

> Then Jesus was led up by the Spirit into the wilderness to be tempted by the devil. He fasted forty days and forty nights and afterwards he was famished. The tempter came and said to him, "If you are the Son of God, command these stones to become loaves of bread." But he answered, "It is written, 'One does not live by bread alone, but by every word that comes from the mouth of God.'" Then the devil took him to the holy city and placed him on the pinnacle of the temple, saying to him, "If you are the Son of God, throw yourself down; for it is written, 'He will command his angles concerning you,' and 'On their hands they will bear you up, so that you will not dash your foot against a stone.'" Jesus said to him, "Again it is written, 'Do not put the Lord your God to the test.'" Again, the devil took him to an exceedingly high mountain and showed him all the kingdoms of the world and their splendor; and he said to him, "All these I will give you, if you will fall down and worship me." Jesus said to him, "Away with you, Satan! for it is written, 'Worship the Lord your God and serve only him.'"

Just like then, the devil will come to us as well and say if you have really been delivered, are obedient, his disciple then do this or do that. To combat such pitfalls and go down the path of being a shoddy steward, Thom thought, all I need to do is quote the Word like Jesus did.

Then Thom thought, "Oh crap, to quote the Word I need to know the Word. That means I can't get away with just going to church on Sundays and calling it good." He became conscious, for the first time in his life that a big piece of the pattern is that to really be a partner with God, to be a good steward you have to have a lifetime commitment to God. Once you decided to put on the uniform of the steward, to have the grateful, disciplined response of your whole person continuing the work Christ began, you can't take it off. Just like the definition Thom found of medieval stewards, when the master puts you in charge, makes you the steward, you're in charge until the master returns. When you're a partner with God, his steward, you're in charge until his return. That was an exhilarating and frightening awareness. He wasn't sure if he should leap for joy or beg for mercy. What he did know was that he needed to know more about the three pitfalls.

Lust of the Flesh

Paul wrote to Timothy that the love of money is a root of all kinds of evil (1 Timothy 6:10). Our unbiblical thinking and selfish desires is the root of our problems. Financial pressure is the fruit that is produced. In other words, Thom thought my checkbook and credit card statements were the thermometer of my spiritual life. My worth as a partner with God is not dependent on the workplace's assessment of my added economic value and how much someone is willing to pay to secure my tailoring services or the right to access my knowledge. If I allow my self-esteem to ride on the roller coaster of employment or unemployment, large bonuses or small bonuses, entrepreneurial reward, or corporate bust, then I'm positioning myself for disappointment, disgust, and depression. If I allow my self-esteem to ride this roller coaster, I'm also putting myself in a setting for self-aggrandizement, false pride, and an inflated ego. Thom considered that was why he was stressing about his finances and his relationship with God and why his "fruits" weren't producing the way he thought they should be producing. Satan, the master counterfeiter, was pummeling him into the bowels of disappointment when he felt broke and rocketing him into the atmosphere of arrogance when the money is bountiful. The lust of the flesh should be resisted at both extremes. Thom's self-worth is a function of who he is in God not what he owns. Thom grasped that it's not about self-worth it's about God-worth!

As the slogan goes, "Have it your way," Thom saw that in today's consumer society you want what you want, and you want to keep everything you believe you have earned. Just like the random reflection Thom had about growing up and stewardship and being the rebellious teenager, you're into taking and not into giving. We rebel against God's plan and principles because our flesh thinks it knows better. One of the reasons we withhold our life, including our resources, our "fruits" from God is we want to do things our own way. Nothing could be farther from the truth. Everything that we have comes from God, all of our talents, our clever ideas, our energy, our very life's breath. We may think we exist and act and produce and acquire apart from God, but we don't.

Proverbs 29:23 says, "A person's pride will bring humiliation, but one who is lowly in spirit will obtain honor (NRSV)." Another reason we withhold our life and substance from God is that we don't trust God to provide for us or take care of us. We trust in our own flesh to produce the fruit of our labors and that will pay for all the happiness and joy we seek. When we trust our own flesh, we trust in someone who is frail, weak, and temporary, no matter how strong and great we may think of ourselves at the moment. When we trust God, however, we put our trust in someone who is powerful, all-knowing, and eternal.

How do you view your financial pressure? Do you think it is your root problem, or would you agree with Scripture that it is a fruit issue that reveals other spiritual problems in your life? Don't focus on the effect. Focus on the cause of your problems-the heart.

Lust of the Eye

Thomas reflected that the stance we take toward God and toward money is determined by our vision. "Good" eyes in this context means singular eyes, eyes that are focused on one object of desire, and it is Christ and his kingdom. A "Bad" eye in this context is informed by Jewish thought that says the evil eye-the bad eye- wanders from God towards things, towards possessions. The evil is miserly, selfish, and greedy. Jesus says if you've got one of those eyes, you might think you're enlightened, but you're actually darkened. You think you're smart, wise, and going down the right road, and you're filling your whole life with darkness.

Your whole existence becomes about making money for the sole purpose of participating in that which you see and like-the earth (possessions). You offer your talents, abilities, and efforts to collect a paycheck that will allow you to claim pieces of the earth. The earth subtly becomes the object of your affection.

To contrast this, Thom found that the Bible describes the spirit of the man as the candle (light) of the Lord (Prov 20:27). The Spirit provides insight. Paul clues us into this phenomenon in Galatians 6:17, which says the flesh (the natural eye) is contrary to the Spirit (the spiritual eye).

Jesus came to reestablish a spiritual connection between God and humanity (to open blind eyes). In the book of John, Jesus asserts that the time has come for true worshippers to worship God in spirit and in truth. There are many ways to worship, but it can be summed up like this: Respect the authority of the Spirit of God. Worship is about reverence and obedience (hearing). Worship implies a proper relationship with God.

Thom realized that, in terms of putting his own financial house in order, getting his piece of the earth, he needs to stop listening to the scam artists that promise big returns with small risks. He must become his own financial consultant and never again invest in anything he doesn't understand. If, as a member of the Christian Middle Class that Thom identified with, buying things has become an additional source of his identity, like when he heads to the mall. When he does that, the Gang of Three is waiting to further derail his life.

Gang member One: self-centeredness gets in the way of our fully enjoying the life that Jesus promised. The Bible term is flesh. When we live in flesh, we can be small, independent, selfish little nasties. One interpretation of flesh is "learned independence from God." In other words, when we live in the flesh after we've committed our live to Christ, we are employing the same strategies we used for survival before we trusted Christ.

Gang member Two: culture employs for the sake of profit. The Biblical term is world-earth. When we are of culture, we get caught up in patterns that gently, slowly, and seductively lead us to confusion and to disaster.

Gang member Three: enemy, our adversary who wants to undo our faith. The Bible term is the devil. We allow outside forces to combine with internal nature to trap us in money and, consequently, to stop us at money and move us towards confusion.

Thom realized that when God touches your heart in salvation, he touches your wallet as well. That only God provides real security and happiness. If my life should revolve around God's purpose, how can I make my money do the same? What does God want me to spend his money on? In getting to know the Word, that piece of the pattern that led him to learn more about shoddy stewardship, Thom found his answer came down to three things: contented living (1 Tim 6:8), giving (2 Cor 8,9), and saving (Prov 13:11).

Pride of Life

Thom knew deep inside that God is sovereign and the Source of his life. He believes in God and trusts him to the best of his abilities. But he rarely gives him a word of thanks. As often as he should, he doesn't praise him or acknowledges his work in his life. Thom thought that most of the good things in his life came with a little bit of luck, hard work and from his own capabilities. Rarely did he praise God for his capabilities, hard work or luck.

God desires our praise not because it satisfies any need in him, but because it opens us up to receive from God. When we praise God, we have a much clearer understanding of who he is, and who we are, and a much greater appreciation of all that he has done for us. Praise keeps us cleansed of pride. It keeps us in a right relationship with God.

In Review

The Lord simply does not prosper to anyone who is rebellious, proud, unbelieving, or unthankful. Such a person has closed herself to God and, therefore, is in no position to receive from God.

It is not enough that you give God your heart, time, energy, talents, and strength. Your material substance is a part of you. In many ways, it is a tangible expression of intangible time, energy, talents, and ability. You have what you hold in your hands because God has given you the ability to earn it; money is earned in exchange for time and skills.

Giving to God opens up the financial area of your life to God. If you want to be blessed financially, you must be generous in your finances. As is true in every other area of life, the degree to which you open up yourself to God in giving is the degree to which you open up yourself to God for receiving. If you are closed to God in your finances, you are also closed to God in reaping financial blessing.

Giving is a mirror, a reflection on your understanding of and relationship with God.

People become interested in giving for one primary reason: Because we are made that way. According to scripture, we discover the very essence and joy of life in the Spirit of the God who gives us all things. Relational theology demands a response. Those who have received grace are compelled, out of the reception of grace, to consider their own giving. Therefore, giving is a biblical imperative, and stewardship is a lens through which Christians view the world.

The devil, enemy, will come to you and say if you have really been delivered do this or do that. But just quote him the Word like Jesus did.

We know that all of us are going to be tempted in the three areas of life.

1. The Lust of the Flesh. Guard your desires. True wealth is cultivated through your core value system.

2. The Lust of the Eyes. Guard your eyes. God increase your blessing according to your level of faith.

3. The Pride of Life. Don't think of yourself as being better than everyone else. Do not allow fear to diminish your potential wealth.

What Thomas discovered about shoddy stewardship is that it is about relationships. The kingdom of God is the kingdom of right relationships. If you do not have the right relationships, you will not be content. Right relationships bring contentment, and that is being truly rich!

Pray

Father, you have given me tasks and responsibilities. And you have also given me the grace to "carry my load" and the Holy Spirit to guide and help me. Give me the strength and the will to respond to you in every moment, to work and serve you and the people you send my way. Amen

Stewardship

Prudence, Prosperity & Knowledge

Work was slow on this particular Wednesday for Thom. So he began to daydream about what the uniform of the steward may look like. His first thoughts were around a traditional steward's coat. The one we're most familiar with today, banded collar, jacket with sleeves, sleeves have bands or chevrons on them. But that wasn't really fitting the pattern he was formulating in his head.

He was fairly sure he had the first piece of pattern with his working definition of what stewardship is:

> Stewardship is the grateful, disciplined response of the whole person continuing the work Christ began. It is dressing ourselves for a life of faithful service as partners in God's creation.

Then it stuck him. A vest!

It's versatile, and adaptable to many situations, just like God's Word. A vest can be worn as part of many diverse types of uniforms. A vest can be worn on formal occasions with a tuxedo at weddings, and black-tie affairs. It can be worn as part of a business uniform, as part of a three-piece suit or a shopkeeper's vest. It's also not limited to a particular fabric. Vests can be made from silk, corduroy, and everything in between. A vest can be a fashion statement or a complimentary piece to a larger ensemble.

Just like a steward may be in charge of many distinct aspects of a household or whatever the master may have left her in charge of, and how God's Word applies to a variety of situations, a vest can be worn in a diversity of occasions and situations. Thomas said to himself, "Basically, a vest is multifunctional, same as God's teaching about stewardship."

Thom could now craft a pattern, a vest, which could be sewn together into a uniform, a uniform he could wear. A uniform that let him be a faithful servant to God. A uniform that let him focus on higher things. A Uniform of the Steward.

Always being the tailor, Thom thought, "What are the threads that comprise the materials, the cloth, to lay my pattern against?"

He knew his journey wasn't done. He needed to continue to discover what the cloth for his uniform was made of. So, after work, back to the library he went.

PRUDENCE

Thom figured he would start with the basics. It had worked well for him so far, so why alter success. He began with the simple question: What is prudence? The definition he came up with was that prudence is skill and good judgment in the use of resources. When applying this definition to stewardship he thought it could mean careful forethought and planning. It would be a habit of prudent stewardship and financial temperance. A habit he thought he would like to pass on to his kids someday. That is, once he had kids. He also thought one of the most precious gifts the Lord entrusts to us is our family. To not provide for their future is to violate his position as their shield and steward to them. He recalled 1 Timothy 5:8 "Each of you should look not only to your own interests, but to the interests of others."

As he contemplated this verse, the notion struck him. We are not called to be saved and then just do nothing. There is work for each of us to do. The Church has been commanded to take the gospel message to the world, and each of us, as a part in the Body of Christ, has been assigned a role in that task.

Reflection: Procrastination lives just around the corner from poverty.

It was getting late for a work night and Thomas headed home. As he got ready for bed, he read his devotional for the day. It was Matthew 7:26–27, and it read, "But everyone who hears these words of mine and does not put them into practice is like a foolish man who built his house on sand. The rains came down, the streams rose, and the winds blew and beat against that house, and it fell with a great crash."

These verses helped tie some things together about prudence for Thom. God doesn't call us to be financial drifters whose financial planning consists merely of balancing our checkbook at the end of the month. This is the equivalent of building our financial homes on sand and will have a detrimental effect on our stewardship and spiritual maturity. You have to attain the ability to be a good steward over every opportunity in order to have the good success that God has promised his people. Stewardship is more than making offerings at church. It also includes a financial portfolio and estate planning that allows you to have the greatest impact with what God has given you. Our goal as believers should not be how wealthy we can be but how well we can be. Wealth and well-being are not always synonymous. As Thom drifted off to sleep, he realized stewardship is more than being a good steward with what God has given him now. It also included how he would be prudent in using his skills and good judgment to provide resources for future generations so that they too could live well and not just be wealthy.

PROSPERITY

The road to biblical prosperity begins on earth, but it ends in heaven.

As Thomas was moving along his journey of discovering what stewardship meant, he wanted to share what he had learned so far with his pastor and get his thoughts. After Sunday services the next week Thom shared his insights. His pastor asked him to be bold and ask God to reveal to him in his Word what he desires for Thomas to take as the next step of growth in his journey toward wise financial stewardship.

Both were intrigued with what the other had to say about the subject. So they decided to continue their conversation over lunch. Thom's pastor shared that the purpose of mastering biblical prosperity and godly stewardship come clearly into focus when we begin to see them not as a means of chasing temporary gain, but as God's plan for us to build upon an eternal foundation. Instead of being doubly deceived by the pursuit of wealth, we begin to understand that biblical prosperity is a means to being doubly blessed, both on earth and in heaven.

When we have out financial house in order, it is no longer an obstacle, distracting us from the Lord's purpose for our lives. Rather, we are free to receive all that he has prepared for us in the Kingdom of God and the Kingdom of Heaven. We are commissioned to go and spread the gospel and be a light to a lost and dying world, all the while storing lasing treasures in heaven.

"So what you are saying Pastor," Thomas said, "Is that prosperity on earth is only a by-product of godly stewardship, a mere shadow of what is to come in heaven. The true product of godly stewardship is eternal treasure."

"That correct, Thom." his pastor said. "The purpose of godly stewardship and biblical prosperity finally is to store treasure in heaven. When we stand before the Lord and eternal treasure will await us. The sum of that treasure will be based on our acts of obedience here on earth. That is why we pursue biblical prosperity; that is why our goal is to be godly stewards."

He continued, "here are some biblical basics for you to consider:

1. Biblical prosperity is impossible without faith.
2. Biblical prosperity is impossible without the willingness to separate.
3. Biblical prosperity is impossible without the tithe.
4. Biblical prosperity is impossible without obedience.
5. Biblical prosperity in impossible without wisdom and knowledge.
6. Biblical prosperity is impossible without humility."

"The Lord's primary purpose for training us in biblical prosperity is to conform us to the character of Christ so that we can rule with him for all eternity.

Thom asked, "So how do we become Christlike stewards?"

The pastor replied, "By understanding this spiritual principle: Godly stewardship is held in a perfect balance between Holy Scripture and the Holy Spirit. The perfect principles of godly stewardship will always be revealed in scripture and confirmed by the Holy Spirit.

Biblical prosperity has three components: godly success, godly affluence and influence, and godly freedom."

Thomas said, "Then the true purpose of stewardship is to glorify God and to prepare us to rule and reign with Christ for eternity."

"Yes, exactly." The pastor said. He went on, "Our eternal purpose on earth is not to amass fleeting wealth, and it is to obtain biblical prosperity. Biblical prosperity is the ongoing process of godly stewardship and is comprised of three foundational concepts I mentioned earlier."

Godly Success

The Lord has a distinct and wonderful plan for every believer's life. You are perfectly created for your unique purpose. When you commit your life to living in the midst of that plan and seek the Lord's direction, something miraculous begins to happen. A supernatural release is placed upon your life. Doors that once were closed spring open, and deeds that were impossible suddenly are done. The Lord revealed the requirement for godly success in Joshua over five thousand years ago, and it remains unchanged to us today.

Do not let this Book of the Law depart from your mouth; meditate on it day and night, so that you may be careful to do everything written in it. Then you will be prosperous and successful (Joshua 1:8).

Godly Affluence and Influence

Having godly affluence and influence is having all of the means necessary to accomplish the Lord's unique purpose for your life. The Lord will never call you and not equip you.

And my God will meet all your needs according to his glorious riches in Christ Jesus (Philippians 4:19).

If you are truly pursuing his plan for your life, the Lord will always bring into your life the funds and the people necessary to help you accomplish the task at hand. But there is a requirement that he will place upon you before releasing affluence and influence into your life.

Seek first his kingdom and his righteousness and all these things will be given to you as well (Matthew 6:33).

Godly Freedom

This is a supernatural release that you receive when you have purpose in your heart to serve God instead of money. It is at this point, when you have chosen to no longer worry about tomorrow, that the supernatural and the miraculous become commonplace in your life. This freedom is not just the absence of fear and anxiety. It is a bold faith born of total dependence on the Lord.

Now the Lord is the Spirit, and where the Spirit of the Lord is, there is freedom (2 Corinthians 3:17).

As their lunch together concluded, the pastor left Thomas with these words, "With biblical prosperity comes the Lord's gifts of the fruit of the Spirit. Look up Galatians 5:22–23 and Proverbs 10:22 and you'll see what I mean."

Thomas was happy he shared his insights with his pastor and gained some great insights from him over the lunch they shared together. As he mulled over the conversation, he considered part of the reason more people don't experience prosperity is that people tend to gravitate towards what is safe, not necessarily what is good. He was guilty of doing the same thing in his own life.

Prosperity is not necessarily a lasting or constant state of being. It is not enough to know to become prosperous in God's eyes; you must also learn how to stay prosperous. It is only as you live in prosperity that you truly can become an outstanding steward of all that God gives you. Keeping prosperity is certainly at the heart of good financial stewardship.

This line of interpretation lead Thom to think, if I am to be careful, thoughtful, and have good planning, I need to be shrewd; as in being far-sighted, astute, pragmatic, and wary. He recalled Jesus' words about being sheep among wolves, to be shrewd as snakes and innocent as doves. Being shrewd doesn't mean ignoring money, nor stopping at money. It means going through money and getting past money to be more involved in more important things.

God doesn't just hand out financial blessing simply because you gave an offering. You need more in place than just faith; you need a willingness to learn how to manage what you are about to receive. God may give it to you, but you have to manage it. Sometimes when learning to manage what God has given you, you go backwards before you are able to move forward. Like when you set up a fabulous budget, then don't follow it. Or you see something that you must, absolutely must have and buy it on impulse. Instead of delaying the gratification, you immediately satisfy it. You experience setbacks. It's part of learning how to manage what you are about to receive. Often times, you will go farther because of the setback and not in spite of it.

The bible is truly clear: God uses money to test your faithfulness as a servant. That is why Jesus talked more about money than he did about either heaven or hell. He said if you have not been trustworthy in handling worldly wealth, who will trust you with true riches. How you manage your money affects how much God can bless your life. When God blesses you, he doesn't have you solely in mind. God will assist you in making wise decisions with your money. As your wealth is multiplied, God's kingdom should be glorified.

KNOWLEDGE

Proverbs 9:10 states, "The fear of the Lord is the beginning of wisdom, and knowledge of the Holy One is understanding." That was the devotional Thomas was reading today. It was perplexing to him. How can fear be the beginning of wisdom?

He discovered the word translated as "fear" can mean several things. It can refer to the terror one feels in a frightening situation (Deuteronomy 2:25). It can mean "respect" in the way a servant fears his master and serves him faithfully (Joshua 24:14). Fear can also denote the reverence or awe a person feels in the presence of greatness (Isaiah 6:5). The fear of the Lord is a combination of all of these.

Knowledge, Thomas thought, is abstract unless it is being used. There is no advantage to having information that is not being used. So we can be informed we should seek God first and establish order in our financial life through changing our overall approach to money, eliminating debt, and crafting a wealth building plan, but until the wheels are in motion there is no change. Therefore, there is no success.

The key question to ask when entertaining advice concerning how to use your money is: Does this agree with God's outlook on money? That is the test. If it does and it is applicable to your situation, implementation will certainly lead to success.

Thomas knows tailoring, he doesn't know money. He knows he needs to find someone who does, he needs to find money partners; certified public accounts, chartered financial analyst, certified financial planners, bankers, real estate experts, and entrepreneurs, people who have demonstrated competency with money resources.

Thom knows he will never be financially free until he seeks instructions on how to shrewdly mange the resource entrusted to him. And beyond that, be willing to actually follow the instructions.

On his to do list for today he would set up some appointments to find and meet with some of his money partners. And the first test he would conduct is to make sure their advice agrees with the principles of the Word of God.

To grasp God's viewpoint toward money, Thomas felt he must spend time in his presence. Like all believers, we must recognize to be successful in this life; owning or possessing the knowledge of God begins in the very presence of God. The Word of God holds the key to everything that is considered good judgment. It explains how to effectively use the resources God gave us.

For Thomas, the fear of the Lord is the beginning of wisdom, and knowledge of the Holy One is understanding came down to one word: prudence. A prudent person is ready to receive instructions and corrections. Proverbs outlines some of the characteristics of a prudent person. A closer examination reveals a prudent person receives instruction, owns knowledge, utilizes knowledge, does not believe everything he or she hears, and is forward looking.

The heart of the prudent acquires knowledge; the ears of the wise seek it out (Proverbs 18:15).

Thomas discovered that the threads that comprise the materials, the cloth, to lay his pattern against are Prudence, Prosperity & Knowledge. And the strands that compromise these threads are careful forethought and planning, godly stewardship, and a willingness to follow instructions.

If you are struggling to pay your monthly bills, worried about your financial future, or do not have a grip on your debt (spending), you need some instructions. Most of all, you need to follow the instructions.

Pray

Lord, my help and salvation, I pray for grace to wait patiently and expectantly for you to visit me with your presence. I seek your face and wait for you to guide me, to instruct me, and to assure me that you are listening and that you will speak. Amen.

Stewardship Trust

As Thomas was going through his to-do list for the day, he was reviewing who he should select for his money partners. Who should he trust to help give him instructions about being a prudent steward with the resource God is entrusting to him? In his stream of consciousness, Thom began wondering about trust. How would he completely trust God on this stewardship journey he is on? What really is trust? Trusting God with money is a scary thing. What if the money runs out? What if the choice is between giving to God and paying the bills? What if, what if, what if?

When the mini panic attack subsided, Thom thought trust is about knowing (fearing) that God will provide for his needs and living it out. To trust God completely, Thom remembered who he is. God is not a stranger to a believer. When he felt like he was failing financially, it was not a group of strangers that was going to catch him. It is God that cares for him. He can provide those things he needs financially. All of it is his anyway, even the money. He is the God who had given his Son as a sacrifice for him. Wouldn't God then give Thom all the things he needs? God is the one who is going to work all things together for his good. Thom thought, I can trust God completely because he is the God who loves me and can provide for me.

When we trust God to control our finances, he will take even a small amount and multiple it for our sufficiency. Thomas recalled many of his fellow church members testifying as to how God has stretched a small salary to care for needs; friends bring food, unique gifts come from unexpected sources, things like that. When we first put God first and give him his due, no matter how little we have, he will honor and bless our faith.

Thomas thought God wants to use us to help meet the needs of others was well. However, we must be willing to be used to be instructed. We may think we don't have much to give or much to offer to God. That is irrelevant. If we have the attitude that whatever we have belongs to God and that he can use it, he will.

God does wonderful things as we respond in obedience to the trying of our faith. For some, the trying of their faith may be to begin tithing, like Thomas was struggling to do. For others, it might be to increase their giving or to purchase with cash only using no credit cards.

Thomas remembered that little is much when God is in it. Don't limit the blessing of God on your life or the lives of others by a lack of willingness to give your time, talent, or money that God has supplied. Let's respond in obedience and faith to the trying of our faith as we seek to be good stewards of what God has entrusted into our care. When we respond in this way, God will bless others and us in ways beyond our expectations and imaginations.

Even when all the "what ifs" come flooding into you, causing doubt, realize that God is always there to take care of you. From last Sunday's lesson, Thom recalled Hebrews 13:5, "I will never desert you, nor will I ever forsake you." Though God allowed the financial situation Thomas is in, he realized that God has not forgotten him and will be there to give him what he needs. Thom realized he has the power to be content through Christ. Philippians 4:13 tells us, "I can do all things through him who strengthens me." Which mean that he is my focus of existence. He is my source of contentment and the One who, through want and abundance, meets my needs. I trust him. He supplies my wants and releases my prosperity in the increments I can handle. It is not because I am such a good sheep. It is that he is the good shepherd that I shall not want.

One of Thomas' things to do for the day was to exercise. So off to the gym he went. As he was taking laps around the track, his mind began to wander about this journey he was on, and some random connections were made. He understands the pattern to use to be a faithful steward, and the cloth it should be made from, and the thread it should be sewn with. The random thoughts he was having is, how do you keep the pieces of the uniform together, how do you keep the cloth strong to prevent it from wearing out or ripping? That's when he made the connection. Exercise.

He grasped God dealt everyone a measure of faith to trust in him. Yet, it seemed to him some people have more faith than others. Then he comprehended that it is because faith is like a muscle and must be exercised. It's like his new stewardship trust; his faith muscles are not yet developed.

The best way to exercise a weak muscle is to expose it to resistance. The trying of our faith are the training tools. When you face a challenging time and God brings you through it, you develop trust that he will bring you through the next crisis. The more resistance training, the stronger the muscle of trust.

Thomas' trainer told him that repetitions bring results. When it comes to building muscles, how much weight you carry is not as important as how many repetitions you do. The more reps, the more you will be strengthened, and the more weight you will eventually be able to bear. If you lift five pounds repeatedly, eventually you will master the five-pound curl and can move on to ten pounds. So, it is with responsibility and growth in the spirit. If you can master trust on one stage, you can master it on another. You begin to understand that if God brought you through that, he could bring you through this.

As you master each stage through repetition, you will find there are stages of success. The just enough stage and the more than enough stage. God will always take care of you. He will give you all that you need for each stage. But the preferred state is a collaborative effort with God. It is crucial that you do not allow your progress to become paralyzed by a lack of trust brought on by a lack of funds-the just enough stage.

We don't want to be just getting by. We don't want to struggle and eke out our exitance. But the reality is that God's strength and purpose is often revealed through our struggles. We tend to savor and appreciate what we earn with our sweat and tears and learn what it is we really want and are willing to work for. Just enough is a stage we need to go through to determine if we have the will and tenacity to go on to the final stage of success and rest comfortably in the more than enough stage.

In Deuteronomy 8 we see a prophetic vision of a delivered, prosperous Israel. The vision was for the time after leaving the arid, barren regions of the wilderness. Their new home would be a good land, "a land of brooks of water, of fountains and depth that spring out of the valleys and hills; a land of wheat, and barley, and vines, and fig trees, and pomegranates; a land of oil olive, and honey; a land wherein thou shalt eat bread without scarceness, thou shalt not lack any thing in it (Deut. 8:7–9)." Israel would move from dryness to fertility, from want to abundance, from meals of boiled, broiled, and baked manna to virtual culinary feast for the eyes and taste buds. God delivered them from "just enough" to a land of plenty. This is where God wants us to be as well. He has the power to have "more than enough." But your seed of greatness will not grow without you using your faith, your stewardship trust, to stretch yourself beyond your past limitations. When you work together with God and put into action the gifts, he gives you, you too will be brought to a place of abundance.

But Deuteronomy 8 does not just give a prophetic insight into Israel's history of deliverance and blessing. No, there is also a warning within the story (see Deut 8:11–14). When you are in a place of plenty, when times are prosperous, you may say to yourself, "My power and the strength of my hands have produced this wealth for me (Deut 8:17)." "But remember the Lord your God, for it is he who gives you the ability to produce wealth, and so confirms his covenant, which he swore to your forefathers, as it is today (Deut 8:18)."

When God makes a promise, he keeps his Word. However, it is often required that we lay hold on to the promise by acting on it in an aggressive way. We must go after it with total abandonment and commitment and know that God's blessings don't necessarily come through the kindness of others.

When our repetitive exercising of trusting God has led us to that stage of more than enough, to a place of abundance we need to think about what he has given us in his abundance. Out of his abundance, God created the world for us to be caretakers of, and what he created was good. Out of his abundance and love for us he gave us his Son, Jesus, so we could be one with him.

It was not the leftover that God gave us, but the abundance. Our commitment back to God should also be out of our abundance and not the leftovers. We give because God has first given to us.

There is no true receiving from God without the balance of giving to God. It's like having a wide-open door that allows passage in both directions.

Each of us has already made commitments out of our abundance, but we may not think of them as such. Our house payments, car payments, cable tv, cell phone, electric bill, etc., are such commitments. These are commitments taken off the top of our paychecks, or the abundance of our paychecks, and not what is left over at the end of the month.

Never forget that it is God who gives us the power to get the wealth

---

As Thomas was heading home from the gym he thought, the question is, why do so many people, including himself, give so little?

The answer he thought, or given to him, was a lack of trust in God and trust instead in themselves. They trusted their own judgment over God's. they believed they knew better than God and what was good for them. And that's the root of sin-trusting in themselves, not God.

The opposite of trust in God is not distrust in God but rather trust in ourselves. We put trust in ourselves because we don't really trust that God's universe has enough resources for us to live if we gave more money to the church.

While having dinner with a friend later that evening, Thom was sharing with her all the connections he had made while exercising. And how he realized that he needs to exercise more on trusting God, on having more faith in him.

Thomas' friend took it all in and listened to him carefully. She saw how Thomas was growing in is faith, how the exercising he was doing was beginning to show results. Then she related this story to Thom to give him her perspective on faith, "I've discovered that there are two kinds of faith. One is what I call buzzard kind of faith. Buzzards out in east Texas are always circling the sky, eye on the ground, never the horizon, looking to feed off the dead, whatever is left over after something else had come along and made the kill. The second kind of faith, the faith that we need to instill in ourselves, is an eagle's kind of faith. And the eagle always gets first shot. An eagle never hesitates. An eagle doesn't waste its time on leftovers or residue. An eagle swoops in with precision and power. We should aim for the eagle's worldview, refusing to settle for mediocrity, insisting on getting the fresh blessings on the front end, not the leftovers on the back end. An eagle's kind of faith is a real threat to the devil. A buzzard's faith is circumstantial at best. The choice is yours Thomas."

Later, in the quiet of the night, Thomas lay in bed contemplating all that had transpired today. He made the connection that God doesn't want a part of your life. He asks for all your heart, all your soul, all your mind, and all your strength. God is not interested in halfhearted commitment, partial obedience, and the leftovers of your time and money. He desires your full devotion, not little bits of your life. He doesn't want buzzard faith; he wants eagle faith.

When we learn to genuinely love God, we will trust him to guide and direct our respective paths. He will ensure we receive enough natural resources in whatever state we find ourselves in to accomplish all those things within his will we have been dreaming of.

Pray

The earth is the Lord's and the fullness thereof. I praise God for endowing me the ideas and bringing me before the contacts I need to generate the resources required for everything I need to fulfill his purpose for my life. Amen.

Purpose of Money

(It's pretty hard to keep from loving the stuff!)

THE NEXT MORNING AS Thom was standing in line, waiting for his coffee order from the local coffee shop, he said a little prayer to himself; Lord, exercise me so that I may have the faith of an eagle. And just then, his order was ready. As he handed the cashier a few dollar bills, the In God We Trust on the back of one of the bills caught his eye. It stuck him, what is the true purpose of money?

A stream of consciousness from high school history lessons flooded his thoughts. He recalled the dollar bill shows the Great Shield of the United States, which contains the American eagle flying free, holding 13 arrows of war in its non-dominant left talon and an olive branch for peace in its dominant right talon. The banner in its beak reads "E Pluribus Unum" meaning "Out of Many, One." The shield's horizontal blue band represents Congress uniting the original 13 colonies. These are represented by 13 red and white vertical stripes. Thirteen stars above the eagle represent a new nation or a constellation in the universe. Red stands for valor, white stands for purity, and blue stands for justice.

On the reverse of the Great Seal stands an unfinished pyramid of 13 rows, symbolizing strength and duration. The first row reads "1776" in Roman numerals. The banner below reads "Novus Ordo Seclorum" which means "A New Order of the Ages." This refers to a new form of government or "the beginning of the new American Era." The all-seeing eye of the Divine is bordered by the phrase "Annuit Coeptis." This means "Providence Has Favored Our Undertakings."

With that Thomas asked Providence to help him in his undertaking. After work, he would begin seeking answers to his coffee question, what is the true purpose of money?

Sitting on the couch that evening with his laptop, well, in his lap, Thom pulled out a twenty-dollar bill. He looked at it. Remembered his history lessons about it. Saw the In God We Trust on it. Nowhere on the bill could he find where it claims to be evil. This twenty-dollar bill can be used to buy a bottle of booze, which can help lead to a ruined life, or to buy a bible for a person who doesn't know the Lord, which can help lead to eternal life. The twenty-dollar bill, in and of itself, has no morality associated with it. In other words, it's the attitude towards our money; and what we do with our money, which counts.

Why then, Thom thought, is money such an emotional topic for us? he considered that and started examining his own feelings towards money. How did he feel when he:

- Discovered he was overdrawn in his checking account?
- Faced with the possibility that he has bills he may never be able to pay?
- Gets a raise or bonus.
- Is told that the repair, or service, is going cost far more than he had anticipated?
- Received an unexpected windfall?

A lack of prosperity causes him to feel discouraged, fearful, doubtful, anxious, and frustrated. Total provision and prosperity cause him to feel elated, joyful, energetic, creative, hopeful, satisfied, and fulfilled.

He thought, emotionally, we deal with money like it is a surprise to God that there is money in the earth. How often did his prayers sound like this, "God, I really need some money to pay these bills. Please send some money my way. Let the money blessings fall down from the sky."

Thomas grasped money is a resource, simple. It is the universal exchange system on the earth. I am sitting on money, wearing money, thinking about money, working for money, and so forth. Money is the one thing we all have in common. We can do next to nothing of physical significance without cash. Money answers all things (Eccl 10:19).

Surfing the web for various definitions of resource, Thomas came up with a working definition for him. A resource is the entire means available for productivity and/or maturity. The resource represents the whole amount available. The resource can do nothing in and of itself. The resource-user does not typically own the resource. The resource serves a distinct purpose-production and/or maturity. In Genesis 1:29 Thom read, we were created to manipulate resources to do what God designed us to do, which is to be productive in the earth.

God knows we need money (resource). He is the one who gave us the talents and abilities to make money. Many of us, however, do not have the right attitude towards money or the way to go about generating it, which in turn leads to mismanagement of resources and dependence on the natural things that God created.

It was getting late, and Thomas would ponder these thoughts as he prepared for bed to see if he could find a resolution in his mind. He would meditate on the Word of God and the purpose of money.

During the night this is what came to Thom: God does not condemn money. He is concerned about our relationship with money. Money is not the principal thing; wisdom or the Word of God is (Prov 4:7). The Holy Spirit counsels us according to the Word of God. Money is the resource that helps us fulfill that which God gives us to accomplish. When we are worried about paying our bills or buying some more stuff, then we are not sensitive to God's purpose concerning us. In fact, if we don't learn to trust God, we will never reach our potential due to the fact we do not have the resources necessary to do what God wants us to with our lives. Consequently, God desires for us to keep our minds on his capabilities and resources, not our own. Remember, he made all resources.

When we talk about trust, we are speaking of a total commitment to and dependence on God. Many of us are committed to our jobs simply because they pay us. We serve our employers because of money. We depend on that paycheck. We get comfortable in our jobs and generate bills that will not allow us to quit even when we realize we are severely out of place and unhappy. It is so subtle, but we exist to make and spend money, not to serve God's purpose for humankind.

Money is important. However, it is your servant, never your master-a means, never an end.

God loves us so much that he wants us to be generous primarily for what it will do for us. The purpose of money is to build relationships. When we give to him, we are strengthening and building our relationship with him. In other words, the generous giving of money can be a spiritual transaction.

There was the answer Thomas was looking for. What is the purpose of money? Money must be seen in the context of relationships and how it can enable our relationships to grow. The purpose of money is to build our relationship with God and with others.

Money cannot give us the intrinsic, internal completeness that we all desire. In cannot lead us to life. Green paper is not power. It has no real worth; it has symbolic worth. Like all the symbolism Thom recalled from looking at the back of that dollar bill, money is what we make of it. Thom thought there are only two choices: (1) we are either the servant of God and the master of money, or (2) we are not.

So, Thomas mulled it over, what's the best way to master money? Then it struck him. Treat it as if you are learning to surf: don't take it too seriously. Make a game of it, a game played to win.

As in any game, there is a beginning stage in which we think, "Hey, this is easy. I should master this quickly." This is followed by the reality stage. When we say, "Wait a minute, this is harder than it looks." Then the last stage when we can compete with the best. We learned the secret: we mastered trivial things and applied them appropriately.

All games have rules and a plan. The rules of our financial game are: (1) know what your opponents are doing, and (2) develop an effective counter-strategy. In this game you are working on one of two plans: (1) your conscious plan, or (2) the culture's conscious plan. The cultural game plan is for you to have a phenomenal front-door income, meaning lots of money coming in, with an unlocked, wide-open back door, meaning lots of money going out. The goal of your opponents is to blind you and bind you. Blind you to true riches and bind you in financial chains. Their tactic is confusion: too much coming at you too fast for you to make good judgments. Your counterstrategy is trustworthy accurate information: What is really happening and how do we turn the tables? We turn the tables by realizing we have families to feed; we are not responsible for feeing sales machines. In other words, we can change the rules. We realize we have enough right now. Our needs are met. We make sure we use that enough in such a way that it moves us into financial confidence and freedom.

We all want to live strong and finish well. That means a growing faith, family, and career. This results in right relationships, which is what the purpose of money is all about.

What is the major obstacle to living the life we want and developing those relationships? Money. What is the minor obstacle? Money. Without the correct use of money, our discipleship, marriages, families, and lives will be impaired. We will end up living okay and finishing mediocre.

Money is called currency because it is meant to flow like the currents of a river. As it flows, some of it will moisten the parched ground of your personal life. Some will flow through to your children and your family. And some will flow through you to bless the ministry that is helping you become all you can be. Remember that God gives the power to get wealth. So, we want to worship not the gift, but the Giver of the gift. The more he blesses you, the more you should bless him and let the currency flow. Our destination is to become truly rich and financially wealthy.

Yet many of us are living with very narrow financial margins. We are one paycheck away from disaster. How long could we live without the flow of income? Any unplanned event (job loss, furnace breakdown, surgery) would crimple our world.

To win the game, to master money, we change what wealth means. Financial wealth means that at a certain age we have developed an appropriate amount of resources/wealth. We have put basic financial practices into place and are financially free. We do not have it all, but we have more than enough.

Thomas came up with seven characteristics that, for him, describe what truly rich and financially wealthy means:

1. You are becoming a generous person in all aspects of life.
2. You are being generous with your money.
3. Your home is paid off.
4. Your kids' educations are funded.
5. You have no debt.
6. You live an appropriate lifestyle (more than enough).
7. You have a pool of conservatively invested money from which living expenses could be drawn five years past your estimated age of death.

Shrewd Christians, thought Thom, do not ignore money, nor do they stop at money. They go through money to get past money, so they can be involved in more important things. Money is in the way. We can't deny it or go around it. We need to go through it to get to freedom.

Money is important to God because money is the chief competition of Jesus. In other words, money can lead us away from God. We will either serve money or we will serve Jesus. Therefore, we do not focus on wealth just for the sake of being wealthy. Money does not determine our significance. But the use of money is intrinsically tied to discipleship. The correct handling of money is critical to living a full life and strengthening and building our relationship with God.

Later in the week Thomas was chatting with some friends after his bible study. He was sharing his insights about what he thought the purpose of money was and how to master it and not be its servant. One of his friends commented on how Thom's insights are radical. Like Jesus' goal to revolutionize the world. He wanted the world to be transformed. How he came to save our lives in their entirely. That means not only our spiritual lives but our financial and relational lives as well, because they relate to who we are.

Another friend added, "Did you know nearly half of the parables of Jesus have to do with money. Money is the subject of more than two thousand verses in the Bible; more than the verses on love and faith combined."

Then one of the associate pastors committed, "Jesus told his disciples, 'I am sending you out like sheep among wolves. Therefore, be shrewd as snakes and as innocent as doves." She continued, "And he gave us a practice to follow that would keep us safe. That practice has two parts. We need to be shrewd as snakes and innocent as doves. These two things work in tandem. If shrewdness is given equal power with innocence, we will be on a straight course to freedom."

"The majority of us have mastered the second half of that equation. We are innocent as doves; we are financially naïve. We are also hard-working, bright people. We are people of faith. We trust people. We even trust the wolves disguised as people; over and over again. We have not mastered the first half of the equation: shrewd as snakes."

With a wink in her eye, she told Thomas, "You keep up your studies and let us know how it's going as you become shrewd as a snake."

Drifting off to sleep that night Thom was thinking about "shrewd as a snake." Most financial trouble is the result of small, incremental lifestyle choices; like the small, incremental actions of a snake. People have been set up by the money game, have very innocently bought into the game, like being mesmerized by a snake's movements, and have been ensnared-like a snake ensnares its prey. He thought we must develop a sense of appropriate toughness, wisdom, and street smarts to navigate the money trap, to avoid being ensnared by the snake. We need to become shrewd. Society has led us to believe that we cannot do this without the help of experts-people purporting to know how to handle money. We have learned that we cannot trust ourselves. That's foolish. We need to change the rules of the game. We are the only ones we should trust with our money. That is, after we have attained shrewdness.

Money is like a boomerang, he said to himself. If you don't toss it out into the flow of God's kingdom, you can't build relationships. Nothing can come back to you. Your level of faith determines the altitude at which your boomerang will soar as it returns to you.

Steps Toward Becoming Shrewd

- The purpose of money is to build our relationship with God and with others.

- More is never enough.
- Money serves us.
- Trivial things mean a lot. If we are faithful in trivial things, big things will be entrusted to us.
- If we cannot handle worldly wealth, we will not become truly rich.
- To get true riches, we must go through, not around or without, money.
- Money is an impostor that promises life but never delivers.
- We must have a plan to attain true riches; we must become shrewd as a snake.

Pray

Father, your gifts are good, and I am grateful for them. Help me, O God, to see only you in the good life you have given me and not to focus on the possessions you have blessed me with. Help me to keep the right perspective on money and prosperity; help me to find joy in the pleasures of living every day simply and quietly so that I can know your presence and hear you when you speak. Amen.

Tithing

As Thomas was finishing going out to lunch with some of his co-workers, one of them said, "Did you know the word tip is really an acronym that means to improve performance." That gave pause for Thom to think, is that what I'm doing with my offering each Sunday, giving God a tip? Shouldn't my offering be my commitment made from gratitude to God in thanksgiving for the gifts that surround me and hold me up every day. Or am I giving a small portion of what I think his service is worth to help him to improve performance in my life? I tip my wait staff 10%—15%, how much should I really be giving to God?

He thought scripture provides us with the principles of stewardship. Then as we seek the Holy Spirit, she breathes life into these principles and imparts them into our spirits; where we are changed to think as the Holy Spirit thinks.

As Thomas studied scripture and researched, tithes kept appearing. He knew a little bit about it, but not much. What he discovered was tithe is an Anglo-Saxon word meaning a tenth. He also learned the offering is what one gives above the tithe. The tithe is the floor of giving, not the ceiling. One can be a giver and not be spirit-filled; however, on cannot be spirit-filled and not be a giver. That God has one plan for giving for his people throughout scriptures, however, this plan has two parts: part one, required giving or the tithe; part two, voluntary giving or sacrificial giving (offerings).

He also found out that there is more than one tithe. When the Mosaic law was instituted, Israel was commanded to give three different tithes averaging twenty to twenty-three percent per year.

The first was a Levitical tithe in which ten percent of everything earned or grown was required to support the Levites and priests as they served in the tabernacle. "I am giving Levi's descendants every tenth part in Israel as their share for the work they do in the tent where I meet with you" (Num 18:21). This tithe was necessary because the Levites could not earn their own livelihood and work in the tabernacle at the same time. It was used to support the national priestly program.

The second annual tithe required was a festival tithe in which ten percent of the remaining nine-tenths of one's income was to be set apart and eaten at the yearly religious festivals in Jerusalem. "Every year be sure you take a tenth of everything that grows from your seed and comes from your field and eat it before the Lord your God at the place he chooses to put his name. Eat the tenth of your fresh grain, wine, and olive oil and the firstborn of your herds and your flock, so that you will learn always to fear the Lord your God." (Deut 14:22-23) This tithe was used to fund the national religious program.

The third tithe the law demanded was a welfare tithe in which, every third year, the second tithe, the festival tithe, was not taken to Jerusalem, but was kept at home to feed the Levites and the poor. This tithe was used to fund the national welfare program. "At the end of every three years bring out the whole tenth part of your crop for that year and deposit it in your towns. Since the Levite has no property assigned to him as you have, he, the foreigner, the orphan, and the widow who are in your towns can come and eat all they want, so that the Lord your God will bless you in everything you do (Deut 14:28-29)."

What Thomas realized is that according to Mosaic law of tithing you must give not ten, but at least twenty percent!

In the New Testament Thom found tithing is used only eight times in the gospels and the letter to the Hebrews. It is used in connection with the tithing of the Pharisees who were fulfilling their obligation to the old covenant. In the book of Hebrews tithing is mentioned in the discussion about Abraham's having paid tithes to Melchizedek (Heb 7:5-9).

What Thomas grasped is that the tithe is our covenant connection between the promises of the Lord and the manifestation of those promises in our lives. Tithing is an issue of trust and obedience. You can trust that the Lord will meet your needs as you obey him. Scripture clearly teaches this principle: If you insist on taking what God did not give to you, God will take back something the he did give you. The simple truth is that tithes and offerings are not an option available to us when we have enough funds. They are the earthly manifestation of one of the Lord's most prevalent themes in Scripture, the spiritual principle of sowing and reaping.

Tithes and offering are the foundation to biblical prosperity and godly stewardship. The faithful giver of tithes and offerings should expect to reap an abundant harvest. Obeying God's command to give tithes and offerings is a key that release supernatural blessings in your life.

When you bring all your tithes and offerings into God's storehouse, you experience the reward of a good reputation. In other words, your life will be enviable. Others will speak well of you and want to be like you.

This relates to your Christian witness. When people see you prospering, they will gravitate towards you. They will want to know your secret. They will want to have the joy you have, the feeling of fulfillment and meaning you enjoy, the blessing that you are experiencing. You will find it easier than ever in your life to share the gospel of Jesus the Christ with others.

Generosity will help you focus on truth, and that will lead you to handle the rest of your income in a wise manner, being shrewd as a snake. However, the main effect is that your insides will begin to work in a new way. You will have more internal godly confidence. You will find that your generosity will expand into other areas of your life, for all the right reasons.

Thomas got it. He shouldn't be tipping God. He should be generous. To be shrewd as a snake, change the rules of the finance game; decide to become generous. Starting now! It is not about what you have or what you are going to get; it is about what you are going to give.

If you can't afford to give, let alone tithe, you can't afford to be truly rich or financially wealthy and you won't enjoy life as God meant you to enjoy it. In other words, you can't afford to be fully alive. Life is found not in the getting or having, but in the giving.

> True stewardship is not simply belief,
> but action on that belief.

We are not becoming generous if we give to get. Giving to get is the antithesis of generosity. That is the error of the Prosperity Gospel. When we give, we should not look out of the corner of our eye for a flood of dollars to wash over us. Our reward is that we have entered God's economy. His economy is different from ours. We will not get a chance to review how our gifts were used until we are in touch with the real reality in heaven.

The truth is the most important part of our financial life is our generosity. God cares about our money not for the sake of our money but because our financial attitudes and actions reflect us as well as our attitude towards God.

For Thomas, generosity means giving at a level that will test his ability to bring blessings to his life. Not that he can buy God's blessing. But giving out of a thankful heart for God's blessings, even when physical and economic life is difficult. Giving in order to say, "Thank You." Giving touches a need in Thom to express his gratitude for the blessings of life.

New Attitude Towards Money

Thomas recognized that our relationship towards money is a matter of focus and how tithing disciplines us to use money properly. Focus comes from the eyes and God holds the vision. Money is merely a resource in the vision. Since we keep treating money as the actual vision, we remain confused and unfulfilled. If our vision only revolves around figuring out how to obtain as much of the stuff, we see around us as fast as humanly possible, we will miss the plan and purpose of God (Matt 6:19-21).

In God's plan it won't do any good to give our money to God unless we give ourselves. Because when we give without giving ourselves to God, when we give out of some other motivation, then we will be tempted to imagine that giving our money is enough, that somehow that will make God pleased with us. Giving just our money can build religious pride, giving things instead of ourselves can easily become our religion, and we never turn to Christ. If we haven't given our life to Christ, we don't need to give our money. God doesn't need money. He doesn't need that at all. Even more, he doesn't want us to delude ourselves into thinking that is what he wants. We give ourselves to God. And when we give ourselves to God in response to grace, then we give our money; but not before.

To grow to spiritual maturity, we need to commit our finances, our money, our resources, to the Lord. There is an axiom. Jesus can have our money and not have our hearts, but he cannot have our hearts without our money. "For where your treasure is, there is your heart also (Matt 6:21)."

With his new attitude towards money and wanting to become generous, Thomas thought if he committed to disciplining himself to give the top ten percent of his income to God, God will help him to be disciplined enough to save.

That was one of Thomas' original goals when he started on this journey. He was worried about his finances and wanted to do better. Learning to save and be disciplined enough to stick to a saving plan would help. With a savings plan he could reap many benefits:

- His joy and satisfaction would increase as he gave to God's work when special needs were presented (There is nothing more rewarding that the freedom to give to God when special needs are brought to your attention).

- He would enjoy financial freedom from the bondage of indebtedness.
- His stress associated with emergency situations that arise would be reduced.
- He will help provide an inheritance for his family.

Thomas knew starting to tithe and a saving plans and remaining disciplined to follow through would be difficult, he would wait until the timing was better. Then he recalled a story his dad told. His dad would start off the story, "Like the preacher who paid a visit to the farmer and asked him, 'If you had two hundred dollars, would you give a hundred dollars to the Lord?' "Sure would." 'If you had two cows, would you give one cow to the Lord?' "Yeah, I would." 'If you had two pigs, would you give one of them to the Lord?' The famer replied, "That's not fair. You know that I have two pigs." His dad would conclude the story by saying, "The whole point is that there is not a better time than now. It will never get easier."

Just then a news story on the TV caught his attention. The newscaster was saying one of the most anticipated events for soldiers who are stationed away from home is mail call. Receiving a parcel is like receiving a box of encouragement. And when one soldier gets a care package from home, it is typical for that solider to share with others the treasures found inside the package. Many families will send extra items just, so the recipient can distribute gifts to comrades.

"Okay, I get it." Thomas said to no one in particular. "Tithing is the same thing as sharing. God entrusts money to us so that we will use it for his kingdom. One of the reasons we tithe is his anger lasts only a moment, but his favor lasts a lifetime (Psalm 30:5). I would rather have lifetime favor from God, than a moment of his anger."

Pray

Father, it is only reasonable I dedicate a portion of my revenues to Your earthly ministry as You seek to reunite with your sons and daughters. You declare in your Word that my giving unleashes spiritual power and protects my natural assets, so I am firmly standing on that Word. Amen.

Putting Stewardship into Action

MARTIN LUTHER ONCE WROTE, "It is easier for God to save a man's soul from hell, than wrestle his hands from his wallet."

God is less interested in what we do with our money and more interested in what our money does to us. Money is a spiritual tool in our lives. It can lead us away from God or can draw us closer to him.

All of us bring unique vantage points and experiences to any given situation. God set it up that way. God is all about interdependence. Just like the way a family is arranged; each has certain assets and liabilities. We are not perfect, and our role is not to act like a handyperson and try to fix everyone. The secret to creating a formidable team is blending each member's unique talents so that the liabilities are minimized. Family relationships are long-term investments. They require much work and vigilant care. But the returns are invaluable.

And family extends beyond those that live under the same roof as us. We are called upon very clearly in the Bible to take care of the poor and to provide for the poor, but the poor are always assumed in the Scriptures to be those who are incapable of taking care of themselves. The poor are nearly always defined as windows and orphans; those who do not have a designated provider within a family structure. The poor, in the Bible, is a classification according to a lack of provider, we are to help those who have nobody else to help them.

Yours, O Lord, is greatness, the power, the glory, the majesty, and the splendor, for everything in heaven and earth is yours (1Chr 29:11). God blesses us to be a blessing to others. He gives so that we might give. As we bless others in need, we are God's instrument of comfort and help. Giving is a means to worship God. Consider the window Jesus pointed out in Luke 21:1-4. God can use our wealth to expand evangelism and discipleship, thereby seeing them go to heaven. God can use our wealth to impact people for eternity. We are to be God's living letters on financial stewardship to others.

Paul Tillich said, "Stewardship begins with receiving, not with giving." To illustrate this point, Paul shared this story:

Simon the Pharisee invited Jesus to lunch one day, a natural act of courtesy for a religious Pharisee. As Jesus entered Simon's house, a sinful woman followed him through the door. She knelt beside him and began to weep. She wept so much, in fact, she washed Jesus' feet with her tears! Then she took down her hair and dried his feet. Earlier that morning she had withdrawn her life savings from the Savings and Loan and purchased an alabaster box of precious ointment. In devotion to Jesus, she broke the box and anointed Jesus' feet.

The act seemed utterly wasteful to Simon, though he didn't have the courage to criticize Jesus for permitting such a display. Instead he thought to himself, "If this man were a prophet, he would know what sort of woman is touching him, for she is a sinner."

Jesus interpreted Simon's perplexed and disgusted glances and said to him, "Simon, I have something to say to you!" Jesus then told a story. Two persons owed a certain man money, one $500 and the other $50. Because neither could pay, the creditor canceled both debts. "Which one of the two men will love the creditor the most?" Jesus asked. Simon thought a while and then answered, "The one, I suppose, to whom he forgave more." Jesus responded quickly, saying, "That's right."

Then Jesus turned to Simon and recited to him the remarkable events of the preceding fifteen minute. He reminded Simon that he should have been the person washing Jesus' feet. He replayed how the sinful woman experienced forgiveness and completely dedicated her life to Jesus. "He who is forgiven little, love little, Jesus said. By implication, the woman first received generously then gave generously!

The world and all its abundance belong to God. What we give back to him, faith, prayer, and personal sacrifice, is the rent we pay for using God's resources.

Like the woman with the alabaster jar, God expects his blessing to flow through us to those around us. The more blessings that flow through us, the more he bestows.

God is far more concerned about our attitudes and desires toward money than he is about our current bank statement. He is far more concerned about how we spend our money and allocate our resources than with our starting and ending balance. Good financial stewards involve overseeing assets and liabilities in a manner which increases net worth. Every time we use a resource, we decide, and that decision reveals what kind of steward we are.

Do What God is Calling You to Do

Part of learning to put stewardship into action is recognizing there are five important ideas that are important to achieving success.

Faith in the Favor of God

Favor will come to your life when you understand who God is and who you are, and when you find your unique purpose in life in the light of God's will. That is why it is important to take advantage of and become a good steward over the things God gave you. He knows what you need, and he know when and through whom to give it in order to enhance his ultimate purpose in your life.

Identify Your Gift

God gives each of us our own unique gifts (our assets and liabilities). It is our job to recognize these gifts, nurture them, and utilize them to live up to our full potential. God gives you the resources for success. It is up to you to recognize them and use them to their fullest. If you faithfully use what God has given you, your gift, you will open the doors you need to succeed.

Power of a Plan

Many of us fail to be good stewards because we have no plan. A plan takes all your resources, your gift, and maximizes them by bringing structure to the concept. A plan puts soil in a pot, plants the seed, and regulates the temperature and watering schedule so that the seed becomes a healthy plant.

A plan for financial success will involve some fundamental changes in your attitude and actions. It will take discipline to make and keep accountable to a budget. It will take steadfast commitment to plant your resources in good ground, in tithe and offerings as well as sound investments. It takes both the spiritual and the practical for you to have good success. The blessings of the Lord make rich and added no sorrow to it (Proverbs 10:22).

So, blessing may bring riches, but it is not riches alone. Riches, without the Father's blessing add much sorrow to life, and that we do not need.

You will need to stay on top of your plan and work it out. It will work if you work it. No plan is successful if it is just a theory. It must be put into action. Your plan should be written out, and it must include specific actions and deadlines to fulfill those actions.

Giving is the Cycle That Release More

The accumulation of wealth should never be your goal. Wealth in the Kingdom in not the end, but the means to the end. The end is that the gospel will be preached to the entire world and broken lives be redeemed and restored. God should be out financial advisor. Just like the supply of manna given to the Israelites in the wilderness, so will be our financial supply. If we take what he gives use it as he commands, the supply will continue. If we are generous, God will continue to be generous to us. But if, like the Israelites, we hoard our supply, we will find that in time it will dry up.

Generosity protects us from falling prey to the sin of serving money. You are not to serve money. Money is to serve you, and you should serve God by using it according to his plan.

Ten Percent is Not Yours but Belongs to God

Pay the tithe to the work of the Kingdom is a key to breaking the temptation to hoarding what we have, and a key to releasing the blessing of God on our life. The tithe reminds us that all we have belongs to God. The tithe is ten percent of our gross income given to support the work of the local church. Our numeric system is based on groups of ten; ten is as high as anyone need to count, as all other numbers are repetitions of the same. When we give God ten percent, we are symbolically saying that all that I have belongs to You. It is the highest honor, as it is the highest number, we can reach without repetition.

Do what God is calling you to do.

- Increase Your faith. When you discover your spiritual gifts and practice them, your own faith increases.
- Become Spiritually Sensitive. When you're spiritually sensitive, you can hear God in other places than your ears.

- Be a Blessing. God's blessing of you is dependent on your willingness to be a blessing. We should want to be a blessing and not just receive a blessing.
- Remember Your Indebtedness. Remember, you're indebted to both God and your previous generation. Your parents and grandparents may have made less money than you; but they managed to lend you money, they prayed for you when you didn't know what prayer was, they sacrificed to get you through school. Honor them, just as you honor God.

It is serving God and money that do not mix. You must choose which one you will serve. We ask God to bless our checkbook, rather than using our checkbook to bless God.

Characteristics of Stewardship in Action

- A biblical steward spends only what is brought home in their paycheck.
- A biblical steward gives generously to the Lord's work starting with their local church.
- A biblical steward has a financial plan.
- A biblical steward understands roles. You will never "get the gold" if you don't understand that God owns it all (Psalm 24:1). You must be a caretaker of what God has given you (1 Corinthians 4:2).
- A biblical steward avoid debt. The rich rule over the poor, and the borrower is servant to the lender (Proverbs 22:7).
- A biblical steward grow savings. He who gathers money little by little makes it grow (Proverbs 13:11).
- A biblical steward practice giving. He who sows sparingly will also reap sparingly, and he who sows bountifully will also reap bountifully (2 Corinthians 9:6–7).

Reflections

Reflecting on all that he had learnt so far and where his journey has and is taking him, Thomas had some solid ideas now about stewardship. He knew that being a steward for God is overseeing something not his as a response to God's love for us. That Stewardship is the grateful, disciplined response of the whole person continuing the work Christ began. It is dressing ourselves for a life of faithful service as partners in God's creation.

He came up with a pattern, a Uniform of the Steward, a uniform that let him be a faithful servant to God. A uniform that let him focus on higher things and that would fit all the pieces together for him about stewardship. That pattern would be a vest because of its versatility.

Thom discovered that the threads that comprise the materials, the cloth, to lay his pattern against are Prudence, Prosperity & Knowledge. And the strands that compromise these threads are careful forethought and planning, godly stewardship, and a willingness to follow instructions.

Thom began to think about a pattern for a vest. He knew it would need at least three pieces; a back, left front side, and a right front side. And maybe a pocket. He knew from his studies so far that the back piece of the pattern is God having our back by giving us his word, found in the Bible, of how to be a good steward.

The front left side would be lessons he is learning from the Old Testament. Like a child growing up he is going through the various stages of maturity. He started his stewardship journey full of wonder, amazement, and lots of questions. Thom feels like a rebellious teen now trying to accept what God is showing him about stewardship. And he is hoping, with God's help to mature into an adult. The Old Testament teaches him to be disciplined, to be a disciple.

The front right side would be lessons he is learning from the New Testament. Once he has matured and become disciplined, he will be ready to receive and practice the lessons of stewardship, the lesson of love.

And, after thinking about it, Thom decides he would add a pocket to the front of the vest. It would remind him that the left hand should not know what the right hand is doing about his offerings. And to remember to give back a small portion, a tithe, to God to show his discipleship to be his steward.

It was all coming together for him now. And he was excited for what lay ahead. He felt comfortable that God did have his back. And he knew he was being a little rebellious, ok a lot rebellious, about what it would take to be a good steward. He knew too that being rebellious was ok, for now. It showed that he was growing, was questioning, was accepting what God was teaching him. Thomas was grateful for that.

Now that Thom knew what his material was made of and how the pattern would lay out on the material, he was excited to start putting his talents as a tailor to use. He already had the back part of the pattern cut out. Now he needed to begin to cut out the front pieces of the pattern. To do that he needed to begin understanding what the Old Testament has to say about stewardship.

And that is where the journey continues...

Pray

Thank you, Father, for giving me unique gifts and abilities. Help me to realize that only I can do the work you have prepared for me to do. I ask for the wisdom and strength to use my gifts for the good of your people and for your honor and glory. Amen.

Old Testament Foundations

Caretakers of this World

It was the beginning of the busy season for Thomas. That time of year when new orders come in for the upcoming season for companies to request new uniforms for their temporary, seasonal, and new hire employees, replace worn out uniforms and changing styles for outdated uniforms. It was also spring and that feeling of newness was in the air. New business, new beginnings, new adventures.

Thom's new adventure was a continuation of his stewardship journey, with a new focus. Or that should be an old focus. A focus on what the Old Testament says about stewardship. As always, Thom began at the beginning—with Genesis.

It didn't take him long to find his first stewardship reference, it was right there in the very first chapter: Genesis Chapter 1 verses 26–28.

> God said, 'Let us make man in our own image, in the likeness of ourselves, and let them be masters of the fish of the sea, the birds of heaven, the cattle, all the wild animals and all the creatures that creep along the ground.' God created man in the image of himself, in the image of God he created him, male and female he created them. God blessed them, saying to them, 'Be fruitful, multiply, fill the earth and subdue it. Be masters of the fish of the sea, the birds of heaven and all the living creatures that move on earth.'

There it was, that old nursery story his parents told him when he was a child about being partners with God in his creation, how the angels kept asking him how's it going, and God would answer, "I don't know, go ask my partners. . ." Here was the biblical foundation for that story. He often wondered about how that story originated. Now he knew. Cool.

By reading further, he saw God's plan for us to be caretakers of this world (Gen 2:8—9:15). How stewardship is first a response to his grace, (Exod 34:1-9) a mission, then money (Exod 35:20-29). Thomas realized mission is more important than money. This is one of the first lessons he learned has a businessperson. Of course, this doesn't diminish, depreciate, or deny the value of money. It is a means by which a portion of God's mission is advanced. Gaining a constructive perspective invites understanding of the relationship between mission and money. It is important to keep an appropriate balance between the two. And it's important to never let money become more important than mission. Money follows a mission, not the reverse.

Thom already feared (understood, respected) parts of Leviticus from his earlier studies. He understood Leviticus begins with one of the Bible's basic assumptions that we should worship and serve God with the resources and possessions he entrusts to us, including our gifts, dedications, and tithes (Lev 27). Thomas further understood God requires us to be holy in every area of life, the environment, each other, and our finances.

Thomas respected the stewardship principles in Leviticus of Jubilee, or economic redemption; tithing and generosity; and the concept of work life balance. This is one of the goals he was also striving to achieve; balance between his work, which was crazy busy right now, and his life.

Something he learned was that over the course of a seven-year cycle, most Israelites that owned property gave about 20% of their yearly income in tithes, plus gifts, and other acts of kindness (Exod 13:1-16; Lev 19:23-25; Num 28-29; Deut 16:9-17). Thomas was still struggling with the concept of cheerfully giving 10% and now he's looking at doubling that! Talk about a challenge!

He learned about other challenges to stewardship in Leviticus like defrauding others (Lev 6:1-7), economic idolatry (Lev 19:4) and idolatry (Lev 26:19,30). Plus the concept of stewardship of the poor (Lev 19:9-10).

Leviticus was a tough read for Thomas. For him, it was like reading his company's employee manual of policies and procedures. Lots of dos and don'ts and dire consequences if you don't properly follow all of those dos and don'ts. What he did recognize was God does not ask of us anything that he has not first done for us. That gave him encouragement to continue on with what seemed like the daunting task of trudging through the rest of the Old Testament. Next up Numbers. He was fore warned that it's like reading a census report. Then Deuteronomy.

If you love God, you show that love by obeying his Word.

As Thom read Deuteronomy, a familiar word stuck him—providence. He recalled that word when he first began this journey and was doing research about the symbols on U.S. currency. Recalling that God alone gives us the power to produce wealth and that problems with money come when we allow ourselves to forget its source; we then are driven to look to false sources of provisions and security. Just has he learned in Leviticus; this is idolatry. Remembering those early lessons, he considered something from John Westly, "He [God] placed you here, not as a proprietor, but as a steward. As such he entrusted you, for a season, with goods of various kinds; but the sole property of these still rests in him." It always seems to circle back to that: God is the proprietor; we are the steward. He is the owner; we are the caretakers.

Thomas saw these lesson again in the story of the window's oil (2 Kgs 4:1–7). When we understand the partnership relationship, God is the owner; we are the caretakers, miraculous things happen. In this story Thomas saw how the partnership relationship is supposed to work. When we are cooperating with God in a joint venture, relying on his power to provide, yet also seizing opportunities for responsible gains, not only are debts paid, but self-sufficiency is also gained. For Thom, he saw parallels between this story and the parable of the talents found in the New Testament (Matt 25:14–30). God entrusts us with a little, as good stewards we seek opportunities to increase it. So that God's mission can be advanced. Mission, then money.

Another piece of the pattern clicked for Thomas. Through the Old Testaments lessons he was studying, God is teaching him, the rebellious teenager, to be obedient. Through obedience he would learn discipline, become a disciple. From discipline he would build character that would give him the courage and confidence to trust God to help him respond with his whole person to continue the work Christ began. To dress himself in the uniform of the steward for a life of faithful service as a partner in God's creation.

Wow! Thomas thought. Not only was that insightful, but that lightning struck really close. It was raining outside and raining good. A thunderstorm had developed while Thom was studying, and he didn't even realize it until the bolt of lightning and clap of thunder stuck. Which was coincidental because he happen to be reading Psalm 24:1, "The earth is the Lord's and everything in it. The world, and all who live in it." Thom paused to consider that passage. What about the earth? I've been focused on the finance angle of stewardship, what about being a good steward to earth itself? He'd been immersed in his bible most of the morning, and, from the grumbling of his tummy it was time for lunch. After he got a bite to eat, he would fire up the laptop and explore his questions about being a good steward to the earth.

As he was wandering around the internet, he stumbled upon the Cornwall Declaration on Environmental Stewardship. It's a statement of environmental stewardship from an ecumenical gathering of religious and intellectual leaders in West Cornwall, Connecticut in October of 1999. It was a bit old, but he thought he would peruse it a bit to see what he could glean from it.

He learned people were created in the image of God, given a privileged place among creatures, and commanded to exercise stewardship over the earth. Humans are moral agents for whom freedom is an essential condition of responsible action. Sound environmental stewardship must attend both to the demand of human well-being and to a divine call for humans to exercise caring dominion over the earth. It affirms that human well-being, and the integrity of creation are not only compatible but also dynamically interdependent realities.

So, Thomas thought, all the lessons I've learned up to now about expectations of the steward, prudence, prosperity, and knowledge goes beyond simply my finances; it applies to all that I do. The whole person continuing all the work Christ began.

Continuing to read the Cornwall statement Thom found humans are called to be fruitful, to bring forth good things from the earth, to join with God in making provision for our temporal well-being, and to enhance the beauty and fruitfulness of the rest of the earth. Our call to fruitfulness, therefore, is not contrary to but mutually complimentary with our call to steward God's gifts. This call implies a serious commitment to fostering the intellectual, moral, and religious habits and practices needed for free economies and genuine care of the environment.

This ties back to the very first verse he discovered about stewardship in Genesis. That through our faithful service we are partners in all of God's creation. Not only finances, all of it.

The Cornwall statement led Thomas to the Action Institute's Environmental Stewardship in the Judeo-Christian Tradition which deals with issues of God's sovereign ownership and of humanity's call to environmental stewardship. Our stewardship under God implies that we are morally accountable to him for treating creation in a manner that best serves the objectives of the kingdom of God.

What Thomas came away with was, we, as God's stewards build up and beautify his creation by extending ourselves to others through deeds of mercy and resource sharing. This reality has enormous implications for the way we allocate our personal wealth and resources. He thought a rhetorical question, if God has made his dwelling in the hearts of his people, shouldn't we devote the same percentage of our treasure to caring for his creation as the Israelites did to adorning the temple?

Being responsible for his finances. Wait, check that, restate it. Being a responsible steward with God's finances and a responsible caretaker for this world, Thomas was feeling overwhelmed. He felt pulled in opposite directions over all of this. Sometimes he wanted to sell all that he owned, join a Christian commune, and live his days in intentional poverty. At other times, he wished he didn't have to think about all of this at all!

He was feeling a bit like Solomon, "Yet when I surveyed all that my hands had done and what I had toiled to achieve, everything was meaningless, a chasing after the wind; nothing was gained under the sun (Ecclesiastes 2:4–11)." Thom was feeling the anguish in the words Solomon used to describe the fruit of the works of his entire life: "meaningless, a chasing after the wind; nothing was gained." Thomas could definitely relate. Then the idea stuck Thom, what Solomon was really trying to tell him was, don't hold on to anything too tightly, it's all on loan.

If it's all on loan, stewardship, then, is a follow-through of our love for God. It is putting into life our commitment to Christ. Continuing the work he began. It is putting into a lifestyle what we believe in our hearts and verbalize with our lips. He recollected someone wisely said: "Stewardship is everything we do after we say, I believe." Recognizing God's ownership is crucial in allowing Christ to become Lord of all that he has on loan to us, our money, our possessions, our environment.

Just then, a crack of lightening hit, and thunder rolled through. It startled Thomas and he sat a little straighter and said out loud, "As thunder follows lightning, giving follows grace. When God's grace touches you, you can't help but respond with generous giving. Give to God what's right; not what's left."

As Thomas was making his way through the Old Testament, he saw this critical connection between faith and finances, Giving to God what's right; not what's left, in Lamentations 3:1–24.

After reflecting on his own poverty in Lamentations 3:17, the poet turns his attention to God, his portion. Depending absolutely on God for his safety and security. The poet does not overlook the fact that humans find security in possessions. God gave us the desire to possess, and the poet is not ashamed to appeal to that desire. But instead of merely refusing to trust in resources and possessions as his refuge, he relocates his resources by clinging to God as his chosen portion.

Thomas recalled from his earlier research John Wesley's comment on resources and possessions, "I value all things only by the price they will bring in eternity." That feeling of being overwhelmed was changing into excitement about investing the time, talent, and resources God has given him this day so that on that day he could hear him say, "Well done good and faithful servant." Who thought a poem about lamenting would cheer a guy up? The rainstorm was beginning to pass, and Thomas saw a rainbow out his window.

Churning inside Thomas' head was the thought about being a good steward today. If being a good steward is a lifestyle, then it goes beyond using God's loaned resources today. It also involves stewarding out legacies and inheritance as he learned in Joshua (Chapters 4, 13–19).

The only investment I ever made which has paid consistently increasing dividends is the money I have given to the Lord. —James Kraft, founder of Kraft Foods

Now, why did that quote pop into my head, Thom wondered. Then he saw the Kraft ® Mac and Cheese box sitting on the counter and realized it was close to dinner time. He'd finish up reading Zephaniah, then cook up that blue box sitting on his kitchen counter.

In Zephaniah 1:1–13 he studied the financial focus of the final judgement. While verses 10–11 identify the financial focus of God's final judgment in the sense that God's wrath is specifically directed against the financial districts of Jerusalem, verses 12–13 reveal that the punishment itself will also be financial in nature. The very wealth God's people have earned in rebellion against him will be used by the Lord as an instrument of their punishment. In chapter 3:19–20 he read about oppression and real-world economics.

Thomas' thoughts on lessons he was learning from the Old Testament were beginning to solidify. Through obedience comes discipline that leads to character. In future study sessions he was going to begin exploring each of these concepts of obedience, discipline, and character to see what else the Old Testament has to say about each of them. But for now, that blue box on the counter was still calling to him, or, at least, to his stomach.

Pray

Lord, help me not to feel burdened when I think about stewarding the earth. Instead, help me to work with you to channel the earth's resources for the good of all. Amen.

That's Obey, Not eBay®

It was a Wednesday night and Thomas was finishing up attending a bible study with one the associate ministers. The minister recalled Thom was doing some research on stewardship and asked him how that was going. Thomas replied, "It's been frustrating and exhilarating, both at the same time. I've learned a lot but still have more to learn. Right now I'm beginning to study the Old Testament and see what stewardship lessons I can glean from it. Would you happen to have any suggestions for me?"

She responded, "Obedience. The first and only commandment. Look up Ecclesiastes, chapter 12, verses 13–14. That sums up our whole duty. Then check out the book of Deuteronomy. You'll discover faith is enacted in obedience and obedience is often represented in our financial choices. You'll also see challenges to obedience, like fear and the dangers of wealth and satisfaction, and creating our own altars. You might even see that stewardship includes more than just finances. It encompasses education, nature, and a whole lot more."

Thomas said, "I just learned that! How stewardship is more than our finances. Thanks for the suggestions."

The associate minister concluded. "Pay attention to what the Bible says about fear. It's one of the biggest hurdles to becoming obedient."

"I sure will." Thomas said as he waved goodbye and left for the evening.

To love your God you must obey my commandments.
John 14:15

With hump day behind him, the rest of the week proceeded as it typically does during this time of year. Last minutes changes to orders, designs, and quantities. This wasn't Thomas' first rodeo, and he understood his customers worries, concerns, and fears. Fear. There's that word again. The associate minister warned about how fear; how it's the biggest hurdle to overcome to become obedient.

As he was doing his studies that night Thom came across a passage about fear.

> "Any fear associated with giving to God's kingdom is irrational. It's on par with a farmer who, out of fear of losing his seed, refuses to plant his fields. As absurd as that may sound, many of us are guilty of hoarding the financial seed that God intends to be sown for the harvest that is to come. And it's all because of fear."

Thomas thought fear is the antithesis of trust; therefore if we live in fear of the future, financially, we suffer from the problem of not putting our trust in God. When you trust in yourself, you trust in someone who is frail, weak, and temporary. No matter how strong and great you may think of yourself at that moment. When you trust in God, however, you put your trust in someone who is all-powerful, all-knowing, and eternal. Just like Proverbs 29:23 states, "A man's pride will bring him low, but the humble in spirit will retain honor."

Thomas found other examples in the Old Testament of people trusting in themselves out of fear and not God (Isa 30:1–3, Jer 4: 17–18, and Prov 16:18) and it never worked out well for them. In studying Deuteronomy, as his minister suggested, he found that instead of trusting in yourself, trust in God. "But thou shalt remember the Lord thy God: for it is he that giveth thee the power to get wealth." (Deut 8:18) And as Deuteronomy 12:5–7 describes, people have a variety of opportunities and options for trusting in God through their giving. Each giver should give as God directs.

It was getting late, and Thomas had to go to work tomorrow. Luckily, tomorrow was Friday, and he could look forward to continuing his pursuits about obedience and stewardship. As he drifted off to sleep, he said this silent prayer to himself, "God, I want to use your resources to the best of my abilities. Show me if there are any areas in my lifestyle or budget where I need to rethink how I'm using what you've given me. I want to be a good manager of all your things so that I can better support your work."

During his workday Thomas kept puzzling on this thought: Only when obedience is in place does blessing show up. Obedience precedes blessing. During his devotions that evening, this came into focus for him as he read the story of Elijah and the widow (1 Kgs 17:7–16). He realized that in this story there are a couple of steps to take to go from obedience to belief. The first step towards obedience is to get belief. The woman believed in the God of Israel long before she thought of giving her last meal to him in obedience. Before obedience happens, God wins our heart. The second step Thom saw in the story is God tested the widow by asking for a smaller need first. Then a light bulb went off for Thomas as he finished the story. The utter assurance that the Lord will perform that which he declares in his word. God always accomplishes that which he promises with such consistency, with such certainty, with such unfailing fidelity, that you can live your life with absolute confidence by being obedient to God. He saw a significant truth that not only leaps right up here in the story of the widow, but keeps popping up repeatedly, like a thread in the cloth, throughout the Old Testament, throughout the New Testament and throughout his experiences: that trusting, being obedient and committing oneself to the Lord and to his word is the key to discovering the truth to God's promise and God's providence. Thomas thought, "Wow, how exciting that is! That by being obedient you begin to unlock God's promise just like the psalmist said in Psalms 37:4, "Delight yourself in the Lord and he will give you the desires of your heart." That God wants to bless us, literally that he wants to prepare a feast for us in the presence of our enemies-the very enemies that would try to destroy us (Psalm 23:5).

During the weekend Thom continued his studies. He forgot how early in the Bible the reference to tithing was made (Gen 41:33–36) and by being obedient, we are honoring God. Thomas giggled when saw that even the ants do it (Proverbs 30:25). Also, in Proverbs 3:9 he read how we do honor God with the first fruits. By obediently giving him our first fruits we are showing him that he is our master, not the fruits; be it money, time, talent, however we define first fruits. If we are giving to God our first fruits, we are taking action to show that our heart is loyal to God. It shows the special bond we have with God. God knows we are giving to him a portion of what we have earned to survive. In that sacrifice, we are trusting God that he will take care of our needs. It also shows we know that our wealth is from God. Our first fruits are not the principal thing; wisdom or the Word of God is (Proverbs 4:7). The Holy Spirit counsels us according to the Word of God. Our first fruits are the resources that helps us fulfill that which God gives us to accomplish. That by being obedient without first fruits, God is able to fulfill the desires our hearts even if and when we struggle financially (Hab 3:17–18).

As Thom persisted with his research in the Old Testament about obedience, he realized that God's gifts are not coincidences or conveniences. They came with responsibilities (Exod 2:1—3:14). and if we don't take these responsibilities seriously, we gamble with upsetting God. In Malachi 3:6-12

Thomas discovers just how upset God can become with those that become disobedient and abandon their responsibilities. What he found was in verse 9 when God said, "You are under a curse-the whole nation of you-because you are robbing me." That word nation, which is emphasized within the verse, in Hebrew is gowy. It is used for the pagan peoples and rarely in the Old Testament does God use that to describe Israel. God typically uses another word. When he speaks of Israel, he calls them my people, in Hebrew ben. In this case he uses the word gowy, or nation because it has the connotations of paganism and being heathen. God is upset with "my people" and is lumping their behavior with the behavior of the people living around them.

So Thomas was thinking, God is swearing and name calling his own people for not being obedient and robbing him of the tithe. Man, I would not want to get God so mad that he would resort to name calling me Thom uttered out loud. Like the old adage goes, he thought, "One cannot be right with God spiritually when he is not honest with God financially."

By the end of Saturday Thomas had wrapped up his studies on obedience. He discovered that to overcome fear, you have to learn to trust in God. To trust in God means to be obedient. By learning to be obedient is the key to discovering the truth to God's promise and God's providence. Through his readings of the Old Testament he came back to the tithe and discovered that the purpose of the tithe is to develop Godly obedience, discipline, and character in us. As we trust and allow God to develop these qualities in our lives, we begin to discover that the floodgates of heaven do in fact open up (Mal 3:10).

Next up for Thomas was to tackle the topic of discipline and how it fits into his working hypothesis of through obedience comes discipline that leads to character.

Pray

Dear Lord, You gave use a planet that is here after millions of years. Please tach me how to hold on to what you have given me. Restore my finances like You redeemed my life. Give me the strategy. I need to reposition myself while I have a chance to be more, see more, and enjoy more of life by listening to the advice and applying into my life. I know You are a God who gives second and third chances, I want one now to begin to reclaim what I am allowing bad information and poor spending habits to steal from me. Thanks for being my accountability partner as my new life begins. Amen.

Disciple, as in Discipline

THOMAS HAD A SHARP vision in his head that to be a steward is to obey the master. To be a follower, a disciple, you had to be disciplined. This was being demonstrated to him over and over again in his Old Testament studies. He began to have inklings that from the Old Testament lessons of obedience and discipline, the New Testament would build upon those foundations. What came next in the New Testament was lessons on love and a desire to care for others and to follow Christ and continue the work he began. But that was getting ahead of himself. He first had to find out what the Old Testament said about being a disciple, to be disciplined.

So what was the first verse Thomas ran across as he began to study discipline? Hebrews 12:11:

> No discipline seemed pleasant at the time, but painful. Later on, however, it produces a harvest of righteousness and peace for those who have been trained by it.

He sure could relate to that statement!

As Thom went through the stories in the Bible, he began to see God is all about preparation and having a plan. He already saw this preparation and planning when he studied obedience and the stewardship of prudence, prosperity, and knowledge. To have a plan meant you had to place things in order. This forces you to decide what comes first, second, third, and so on. Thomas had already learned that he wanted to place God first and was learning how to do that on his stewardship journey.

Thomas realized there is an excellent example of preparing and planning; to place things in order so other things may flow from previous planning steps. It was right there in the creation story! First, God needed the true Light to restore order in the earth, which was in a state of chaos. Second, he needed to shape the earth, which was "without form." Third, he had to separate the water from the dry land in order for it to bring forth vegetation. Fourth, once vegetation was present it needed natural light to grow. Fifth, now that there was natural light, the creation of both the sea and the sky could come forth. Six, now that vegetation was sprouting, the creatures of the earth could come forth. Lastly, God rested because he gave everything to us. And why, as God's stewards, we dress ourselves for a life of faithful service as partners in his creation.

By keeping our part of the bargain, being good stewards, we are blessed so we can be a blessing (Exod 19:5–6). It is God's way of raising us into the likeness of his Son.

Thom began to realize that God's discipline is taught through the relationship of giving. He found that the book of Deuteronomy highlights this notion of God's giving and our giving in response. Some form of the verb to give occurs 167 times in Deuteronomy, with God the subject of the verb on 131 of those occasions. He saw the relationship between God and his chosen people ideally was to follow this pattern: God blesses them with gifts. They, to acknowledge their dependance and gratitude, respond by a willingness to relinquish a share of those blessing with others. When they do so, God blesses them again; they then respond once more.

Because of God's longing for a relationship and his people's lack of faith and trust in him, he created the tithe to re-establish, re-enforce, and remember his covenant with his people. Tithing was given as a means for the people to remember God's faithfulness. As the people brough their tithes, they committed themselves again to God's blessing and purposes in covenant and creation. For this reason, tithing became part of the worship pattern of ancient Israel. How did one stay in touch with God's faithfulness? How did one respond in order to experience the benefits of the covenant? Faithfulness, joyful obedience, grateful tithing, and committed discipline.

This reminded Thomas of the lessons he learned while studying prudence. The mark of operating prudently is dealing with knowledge which simply means our words and actions reflect the things we know to be true. Just like what he read in Proverbs 13:16:

> Every prudent man dealth with knowledge: but the fool layeth open his folly.

The signs of a prudent person will reveal itself in a person's willingness to use knowledge and, more importantly, build on it as Proverbs 14:15 points out:

A simple man believes anything, but a prudent man gives thought to his steps.

The prudent person confirms the things other say with the Word of God. When our words are not God's words, we will not and should not expect to receive God's things. Good judgment and foresight comes directly from the Word of God. All words that are not in agreement with the Word result in folly. A prudent man predicts the evil, and hides himself: but the simple pass on, and are punished (Proverbs 22:3).

When we decide to discipline ourselves to exercise good by mediating on the Word of God, we begin to see "the evil" and choose to avoid it. Thomas thought the crux of the matter is that you have to do the dirty work of disciplining yourself, obeying God's Word, following his Covenant, determining what goes first, second, and so forth, in order to receive his blessings to be a blessing to others.

We will never make it into relationship with God if we are not willing to change according to the Word of God. The words from Hebrews 12:11 came back to mind and Thomas uttered to himself, "Man, this is hard."

By being prudent, paying attention, means that we will not let impulsiveness (opposite of discipline) cause us to neglect or squander God's blessings. By being a disciple, being disciplined, we are not short-changing God and the actions we take as a disciple make us truly generous. We do not become generous if we give to get. Giving to get is the antithesis of generosity. That is the error of the Prosperity Gospel. When we give, we should not look out of the corner of our eye for a flood of dollars to wash over us. Our reward is that we have disciplined ourselves to enter into God's economy. His economy is different from ours.

HISTORY OF THE TITHE: CONDENSED VERSION

Thomas was mulling over a few things in his head; preparations, planning, being disciplined. How does one go about accomplishing all of this? Then it struck him. God already has a plan and is preparing us to be disciplined. He does it through tithing. Great! he thought. One more expense I can't afford. How am I supposed to come up with ten percent of my earning to give to the Church? I'm struggling to make ends meet now. Then he calmed himself and realized that was fear and self-doubt creeping in. How quickly he forgot all that he had learned so far and how fast the fear welled up inside him. Being a steward, a disciple, was hard, really hard.

With a breath of fresh air and a calmed mind, Thom set about exploring how did the tithe came about. The first thing he learned was the custom of giving to God 1/10th of one's possessions in recognition of him as lord of the land and in thankfulness of his blessing (Lev 27:30-33, Num 18:20-32, Deut 14:22-29, Gen 28:20-22).

And it didn't stop at 1/10th. What he discovered was there were three tithes (Lev 27). The first tithe was collected annually for the priest. This was called the Levite's tithe or the Lord's tithe (Lev 27:30). This was used to support the priest and meet the expenses of carrying on the temple operations. Then there was the Festival tithe (Deut 12:10-11). It was used for religious celebrations, to bring family and friends together. The third tithe was the Poor tithe (Deut 14:28-29). This tithe was collected for the poor, widows, and orphans.

And these three tithes didn't cover free will offerings that were given for special projects or offerings for the Jubilee celebration (Lev 25:1-55; 27:16-25; Num 36:4). Mandatory tithes equaled between 23-25 percent of annual income. When free will offerings are included, it meant that people were giving between 27-40 percent of their income.

What Thomas concluded is the ideal in the Old Testament was grace giving, whether it was mandatory or voluntary. Giving was meant to come from the heart. It was meant to be offered to God with boundless joy and rejoicing. When you respond with your heart, committing 27 to 40 percent becomes a very substantial part of your income. This grace giving is a privilege that each of us participate in as an act of loving worship to God. It shows we are obedient to him and discipline to follow his Word. By disciplining ourselves to follow the Old Testament lessons we are preparing ourselves to build a New Testament character of gratitude inspired generosity; to give cheerfully out of the abundance which God has blessed us.

Thom was snacking on an apple, processing all that he had discovered about the Old Testament tithe. And it was a lot. Not only in data, but also in commitment. If he were an Israelite back in the day, a third to a half of his income would be a huge commitment and takes a lot of discipline to meet that commitment. No wonder you have to prepare and have a plan. So when you put God first, you know exactly what comes second, third, and fourth. He then had the thought that his discipline commitment was also like as investment into God's work. Just like he discovered before: Stewardship is the grateful, discipline response of the whole person continuing the work Christ began. Like the apple seed he just spit out.

That apple seed represents an investment. And that apple seed has even more seeds in it, and those seeds have even more seeds in them. Thomas began to daydream about if that one seed represented just his portion of his grace giving, what would happen if he planted that one apple seed instead of spitting it out. Say that seed grew into one tree with fifty apples; each apple had five seeds; he would then have 250 apple seeds. If he planted those 250 seeds, he would have an orchard that had 62,500 apple seeds. And if he planted all of those seeds, he would have an astounding 15,625,000 apple seeds! All from that first seed he planted instead of throwing it away. Wow! That is pretty impressive. It also made Thomas feel not so overwhelmed or intimidated by disciplining himself to plan to tithe. If God could do so much with a tiny apple seed, Thom thought, what could he do with my tithe?

ABOUT THE TITHE

Thomas was intrigued; he wanted to know more about what the tithe was all about. He understood that tithing was not a ticket to heaven, it is a disciplined way of participating in the kingdom of God. He saw Jacob first referenced tithing in Genesis 20:20–22. Tithing again is mentioned when Moses instructs the Israelites to use their tithe to purchase food and drink to worship God in Deuteronomy 14:23–26. He was beginning to understand that the point of our own giving isn't the percentage so much as the perspective. He got that tithe is the biblical term that means a tenth and this is a tenth of his gross income. He figured if the government gets it cut off the gross, God deserves the same. He got that the tithe goes to his home church and used to support the ministry of the church, just like his example of the apple seed at work.

The tithe is about a small percentage of all that God has given him and is symbolic of the whole belonging to God. Taking the tithe off the top of his income keeps the proper perspective on who owns all that he has. It was about tithing willingly and happily. Thomas was thinking God doesn't want him to have the attitude that he is cutting a deal with God or paying off the church. God wants gifts given out of a heart of gratitude, obedience, and trust. A generous heart will not flinch at the idea of tithing and will always find that it gives way beyond the ten percent.

Tithing is about the work of the Kingdom and is a key to breaking the temptation to hoarding what we have and a key to releasing the blessings of God in our life. The tithe reminds us that all we have belongs to God.

Then Thom realized our numeric system is based on groups of ten; ten is as high as we need to count, all other numbers are repetitions of the same. When we give God ten percent, we are symbolically saying that all that we have belongs to God. It is the highest honor, as it is the highest number we can reach without repetition. When we give the tithe, we not only honor

God, but we let him know that our commitment to his work is greater than our commitment to money.

That's what the tithe is really all about Thomas thought; obeying God's Word, disciplining ourselves to putting God first, to help us build a character that shows our loyalty to the One who is sovereign over our lives. This same thought was reflected in Hosea 6:6, I want love and not just sacrifice; I want you to know God and not just bring burnt offerings.

With this revelation Thomas reflected on what is had learned so far about what the tithe was all about. He had learned:

- At no time in scripture is the first tenth considered to belong rightfully to anyone other than God.
- We are to make our gifts regularly.
- We are to make our gifts joyfully.
- We are to bring our gifts into God's storehouse, where we participate in the worship of the Lord.

Your bank and credit card statements are theological documents. They tell who and what you worship. With the price of everything else going up these days, aren't you glad the Lord hasn't increased the tithe 15%?

He was also learning how tithing develops his character. By bringing his tithes and offerings into God's storehouse, he was learning to experience the reward of a good reputation; how others were speaking well of him and wanted to be like him. This was correlating to the Christian witness he wanted to develop. As people saw him prospering, they will gravitate towards him. They will want to know his secret. They will want to have the joy he was discovering, the feeling of fulfillment and meaning he was cultivating, the blessings that he was experiencing. He was hoping this would make it easier in his life to share the gospel of Christ with others. Just like others he discovered in his studies that were also tithers. Like Zig Ziglar, Jack Canfield, Jim Rohn, and Brian Tracy also talk about relying on and trusting God. He read from Catherine Ponder, the bestselling author on the subject of prosperity, many of this county's millionaires attribute their wealth to tithing: the Rockefellers, the Heinz, Quaker Oats, and Kraft people.

What Thom was learning about the tithe is that poverty of purpose is far worse that poverty of purse. He wanted to fulfill God's purpose with his tithe. With the tithe God begins to remove our hands from our hearts and our thoughts from ourselves, simultaneously transforming our spirit and our flesh through this single act of obedience.

It was a productive night of studying for Thomas and he felt accomplished that he had learned so much about the history of tithing and what it was about. He began to look at tithing as a privilege rather than an obligation. That was something he would explore next, tithing as a privilege. That night, as he went to sleep, he said this prayer to himself, "God, help me to consistently pray about, when, where, and how much you want me to give."

THE POSITIVE PRIVILEGE OF TITHING

It had been a remarkably busy week at work and Thomas was glad it was finally the weekend. He was looking forward to his morning hike with a few friends. The change of scenery and the exercise would both do him good. It also would be nice to catch up with his friends and chat about what they were up to.

About a third of the way through their hike, one of Thom's friend asked how his research on stewardship was going and what he had learned so far. He caught up with his breakthroughs on what he thought stewardship meant and how he was now studying the Old Testament and in particular tithing. He heard the moans and ughs of his friends when he uttered the word tithing.

So he shared with them how he has observed that some people struggle with the concept of tithing. "Usually, the only reason people ever struggle over tithing," Thomas said, "is simply because they do not completely understand the concept." he started with the basics of tithe means one tenth. He shared with his friends his aha moment that our numeric system is based on groups of ten; ten is actually as high as anyone need to count, as all other numbers are repetitions of the same. "When we give God ten percent, we are symbolically saying that all that I have belongs to You. It is the highest honor, as it is the highest number we can reach without repetition. Tithing is devoting the first tenth of your income to God and his Kingdom." he said, "Look at Leviticus 27:30–33, 'All tithes of the land, levied on the produce of the earth or the fruits of the trees, belong to Yahweh; they are consecrated to Yahweh. If a man wishes to redeem part of his tithe, he must add one-fifth to its value. In all tithes of flock or herd, the tenth animal of all that pass under the herdsman's staff shall be a thing consecrated to Yahweh; there must be no picking out of good and bad, no substitution. If substitution takes place, both the animal and its substitute shall be things consecrated without possibility of redemption.' Look at what the word of the Lord says-that tithing begins at 10%. Not that we should work up to 10% as if it where some kind of goal to achieve. Moreover, that if we do not begin at 10%, we want to redeem part of what God commands, then he wants a fifth or 20% added to it. In banker's terms, that's a 20% interest rate on the loan we are taking from God."

His friends could tell Thom was really into this now as he continued, "You do not tithe just because it is written in the Law that you must tithe, even though that is not a bad reason. However, tithing the first fruits of your income has always been part of God's economic plan, long before the Law was ever handed down to Moses. Melchizedek, the king of Salem, was also a priest of the most high God (Genesis 14 and Hebrews 7). Abraham paid tithe to that high priest in approximately 1883 B.C.—over 425 years before the Law was ever given to Moses. That 4,000-year-old example is to be followed by us today as we give our gifts to God, of whom the Scriptures declare: You are a priest forever with the rank of Melchizedek (Hebrews 7:20)."

Thomas related the story of Jacob, when confronted by God in his "ladder-day" experience at Bethel, vowed two things to God: (1) I will choose Yahweh as my God. (2) I will give you back a tenth of everything you give me (Gen 28:21-22).

He continued, "When it became necessary for the Law to be written down, God certainly never overlooked the beautiful concept of tithing."

"You must tithe all of your crops every year. . .this applies to your tithe of grain, new wine, olive oil and firstborn of your flocks and herds. The purpose of tithing is to teach you always to put God first in your lives (Deut 14:22-23). God does not need your tithe; he created and blessed us with all that we have. He uses the tithe to teach us principles and obedience to the word of God. It is an expression of our sacrifice and worship to him. The tithe proves our creditability of faith. We may say we are disciples of Christ with our tongues but if we do not have discipline in our finances by putting God first and obeying his command to render him his tenth, how can our words ring true? One of the description of stewardship I ran across is assuming the posture of one who serves. How can we truly be in service to God if we are selecting which commands to be obedient to? Paying him should be a priority more than anything else." he asked his friends, "Are you paying God what is right or are you giving God what is left?" They never got the chance to answer as Thom was definitely in sermon mode now as he continued, "When we give the tithe, we not only honor God but we let him know that our commitment to his work is greater than our commitment to money."

"Every place God commands tithing he balances it by promising that if you put him first, he will see to it that your needs will be met by his sufficiency! Solomon attested to that principle nearly 500 years after the Law was written."

"Honor the Lord by giving him the first part of all your income, and he will fill your barns with wheat and barley and overflow your wine vats with the finest wines (Proverbs 3:9-10)."

"In everything you do, put God first and he will direct you and crown your efforts with success (Proverbs 3:6)."

Thom was on a roll as he continued, "Less than 400 years before Christ was born, the Hebrew people had forgotten God's commands. To put it plainly, they had made an absolute mess out of their lives and their nation. They had changed. But the prophet Malachi appeared to remind them that God does not change: before the Law, in the Law, or after the Law."

"For I am the Lord-I do not change . . . though you have scorned my laws from earliest time, yet you may still return to me . . . Come and I will forgive you. But you say, 'We have never even gone away!' Will a man rob God? Surely not! And yet, you have robbed me. 'What do you mean? When did we ever rob you?' You have robbed me of the tithes and offerings due to me. And so, the awesome curse of God is cursing you, for your whole nation has been robbing me. Bring all the tithes into the storehouse so that there will be enough food in my Temple; if you do, I will open up the windows of heaven for you and pour out a blessing so great you won't have room enough to take it in! Try it! Let me prove it to you! Your crops will be large, for I will guard them from insects and plagues. Your grapes won't shrivel away before they ripen,' say the Lord of Hosts. 'And all nations will call you blessed for you will be a land sparkling with happiness.' These are the promises of the Lord of Hosts" (Mal 3:6-12).

And with that the hikers found themselves back in the parking lot where they began their hike. The hike had finished and so had Thomas.

"Wow Thom, that is a lot of information. Sure did make the hike fly by." One of his friends said. Another chimed in, "Yeah Thom, you sure are into this stuff." Thomas apologized for rambling and dominating the conversation. He shared with them how excited he is finding this stewardship journey, and he hoped that what he shared was interesting and not boring for them. His friends assured him they indeed found it interesting and insightful. They even went so far as to say it did help them see how tithing could be a positive privilege. With that Thomas was a glow as he headed home.

In Review

In God's economy:

- He is the owner of all things through creation and redemption.
- We are his stewards.
- We are to discipline ourselves to obediently return a portion of our blessing to him.
- We are responsible to God, the owner, and to society for the management of his creation.
- Faithfulness in this stewardship will bring blessing and prosperity. Unfaithfulness will bring curse and tragedy.

Actions You Can Take

- Choose someone close to you whom you trust and ask that person to hold you accountable as you practice disciplining yourself to be generous.
- Each day pray that God will show you what, where and how to be generous.
- Share with your trusted confidence your preparations and plans to be generous and ask this person to share in your journey by encouraging you and supporting your efforts.

Pray

God, thank you for sending your Son to bring wholeness to the world-to preach, to heal, to deliver and to comfort. Mold me into a worthy disciple and give me the grace to imitate Jesus as the Great Steward of your unbounded love and mercy, to make his mission my mission and to proclaim, in my words and action, that he is the Savior. Amen.

Character

> A good name is more desirable that great riches;
> to be esteemed is better that silver or gold.
>
> PROVERBS 21:1

AS THOMAS WAS LEARNING, character is developed by obedience that comes through discipline. No shortcuts, no amount of money, can reverse this principle. Character development simply takes time. "What are some of the building blocks, or social capital, needed to be an effective, positive, productive member of society," he wondered. He jotted down a quick list that included work ethic, responsibility, manners, sacrifice, stewardship of course, teachability, accountability, loyalty, integrity, honesty, discipline, endurance, courage, honor, and self-esteem. He realized that you could have social capital without spiritual capital, it seems that long-term motivation for social capital flows from spiritual capital, from principles. Just like Proverbs 11:28 says, "Whoever trusts in his riches will fall, but the righteous will thrive like a green leaf."

> A simple man believes anything, but a prudent man gives thought to his steps.
> Proverbs 14:14

The Word of God holds the key to everything that is considered good judgement that build character. It explains how to effectively use the resources God gave us. It's how we can tie prudence to his Word. Thom discovered the book of Proverbs outlines some of the characteristics of a prudent person. A closer examination reveals a prudent person receives instruction, owns knowledge, utilizes knowledge, does not believe everything he or she hears, and is forward looking. He realized a prudent person is ready to receive instructions and corrections (obedience and discipline), which all leads to having a good character.

Before diving too deep into Proverbs, Thomas went back to the beginning; to Genesis 1:26-28. Here he read how we received our destiny or our purpose. That purpose is to be God's representatives, steward, to have fellowship with him and to operate just like he operates; to be his partners. To be his partners, to operate like him, we need to follow his operation manual. Which is to first think the Word, then, speak the Word, finally, the Holy Spirit facilitates what is spoken. In Genesis 9:11-12 Thom saw how this all came to together with Noah with the covenant God made with him.

This got Thomas thinking about resources. How God put Adam and Eve in charge of the Garden of Eden, resources. Noah was in charge of all the animals on the Ark, resources. Again, Thom thought he had a working knowledge of the word and wanted something a bit more concrete. Having done a little research, (i.e., Googling) he came up with this: a resource is the entire means available for the purpose of productivity and/or maturity. The resource represents the whole amount available. The resource can do nothing in and of itself. The resources-user does typically not own the resource. The resource serves a distinct purpose-production and/or maturity. Genesis 1:29 points out we are created to manipulate resources to do what God designed us to do, which is to be productive in the earth.

Thomas was recognizing that to have a good character he should be motivated to see his life as God sees it, then do what God is instructing and guiding him to. Psalm 25:4-5 summed it up for him:

> Show me Your ways, O Lord;
> Teach me Your paths.
> Lead me in Your truth and teach me,
> For You are the God of my salvation;
> On You I wait all the day.

Thomas jumped back over to Proverbs 3:9-10, which talks about honor and first fruits. Honor was part of the list he jotted down and first fruits ties back to what he was learning about tithing. He recalled honor in the bible translates to mean to be wealthy towards God. That first fruits expresses both gratitude and faith. Both part of learning to be obedient and disciplined he needed to have a good character.

Thomas began jumping around his bible, looking at various verses to see how they could tie into what he was learning about building a good character. In Joshua 1:8 Thom discovered God will never call you and not equip you. He will give you the means necessary to accomplish his unique purpose for your life. What he began to see is God delights in a generous spirit but finds his greatest pleasure in giving. We are at our best when we are giving. Thom made the connection that we are most like God when we are giving. That is one of the keys to being his partner and having a good character.

> You have not lived until you have done something for someone who can never repay you.
> —John Bunyan, 1688

God blesses us so that we can be a blessing to others. He does not give us more resources primarily to increase our standard of living, but to increase our standard of giving. Thomas was becoming enlighten to what God was calling him to do in his stewardship journey. What started out as, being worried about his finances and stressing about how concentrating on trying to become financially secure is affecting his relationship with God, is now focused, not on his worries, but God's purpose for him. It's now about his grateful, discipline response of his whole person continuing the work Christ began. It is dressing himself for a life of faithful service as a partner in God's creation.

To that end, Thomas came up with a challenge for himself. He knows he's not a regular giver. So he was going to try an experiment. He was going to give to his church regularly for one month. Then pray and ask the Holy Spirit (part three of the Operation Manual) to show him how this experiment has affected his relationship with God. This would definitely test his obedience, see how disciplined he really was and see if he could begin to build a better character for himself.

As Proverbs 15:5 taught Thomas, "A fool spurns his father's discipline, but whoever heeds correction shows prudence."

A WORD ABOUT DEBT

Okay, more than a word.

Thomas' experiment was proving a bit more challenging than expected. He was struggling to pay his bills, worrying more about his financial future, and was not getting a good grip on his spending (debt). He was in need of more instructions. Most of all he needed to begin following those instructions. He was having the thought that he was in debt because he was lacking forethought for the future. He was familiar with stories about how people are in debt because they lose a job or miss work due to an illness or injury. That wasn't him. He was struggling to get his debt under control. He knew from his studies how he should be putting first things first, saving a position of his earnings, so he could have a financial cushion. He got the message from Proverbs 13:22 that a person who lack forethought for the future leaves no inheritance. He knew God was using these difficult financial situations as a mirror to help him see who he is really. The message of Proverbs 22:7 was ringing loud and clear in his ears.

> The rich rule over the poor, and the borrower is servant to the lender.

Thomas knows that God does not want his people to be in debt. The only thing we are to owe others is our love, which we are to give freely and in tangible forms. We are to be givers, not borrowers. As Psalm 37:21 shows, we have an obligation to pay our debts. And God will help us pay them if we will turn to him and trust him for the wisdom about how to pay our debts.

Thom knew he was backsliding, that God wants him to understand his financial situation and to take charge of it. God wants him delivered from the bondage of constant financial worry and fear and free to use his time and talents for the glory of God's kingdom.

CHARACTER TRAINER

It's back to the tithe.

> Remember the Lord your God, for it is he who gives you the ability to produce wealth.
> Deuteronomy 8:18

For Thomas, it came back to the tithe. When you tithe, you release inhibiting shackles, becoming free to be more sensitive to God's leadership. Thom knew he needed to give freely, give of his money, his time, his teachings, his leadership, his energy. If God is willing to give 100% of Himself for Thomas, Thom needed to be willing to give 10% of himself for God. Thom needed to change the question he was asking himself from, "Lord, what do you want me to do with my money?" To restating it to, "Lord, what do you want me to do with Your money?"

Then it hit him. By being obedient first to think the Word, then disciplined to speak the Word, the Holy Spirit will facilitate him having a good character. His whole existence becomes about making money for the sole purpose of participating, being a giver, in that which you see and like: God's Kingdom on earth. He offers his talents, abilities, and efforts to collect a paycheck that will allow him to claim pieces of the earth. The earth subtly becomes the objects of his affection. What he was realizing, and reinforcing is that stewardship is not only about money, but also about the earth, as he learned in Cornwall Declaration on Environmental Stewardship and the people on the earth. Stewardship truly does touch all of God's resources and is a way of life.

As Thom delved deeper into this stream of consciousness, he found the bible describes the spirit of the man as the candle or light of the Lord (Prov 20:27). The Spirit provides insight. Paul talks about this phenomenon in Galatians 6:17, which says the flesh (the natural eye) is contrary to the Spirit (the spiritual eye). All those lessons he learned about lust of the flesh, lust of the eye, and pride of life came flooding back to him. He remembered Jesus came to reestablish a spiritual connection between God and humankind. (i.e., to open the blind eyes) in the book of John, Jesus' assets that the time has come for true worshipper to worship God in spirit and in truth. Thom knew there a many ways to worship, but he could sum it up like this: Respect the authority of the Spirit of God. Worship is about reverence and obedience. Worship implies a proper relationship with God, a good character.

The answer Thomas was looking for to help him get a grip on his spend was found in Habakkuk 3:1–19. The book of Habakkuk introduced to him the concepts that illustrate stewardship theme of delayed gratification. What he grasped was a life devoted to things is a dead life, a stump; a God-shaped life is a flourishing tree (Proverbs 11:28). From that tree comes the Lord's gifts of the fruit of the Spirit: But the fruit of the Spirit is love, joy, peace, patience, kindness, goodness, faithfulness, gentleness, and self-control (Gal 5:22–23). And in Jeremiah 17:7–8 he discovered the water for that tree is equivalent to discipleship to God and the fruit is stewardship and tithing.

Thomas understood that victory over his worry about his finances comes through surrender, that it's not his, it's His. As Psalm 50:7, 9–12 puts it:

> I am God, your God...
> I have no need of a bull from your stall or goats from your pens,
> For every animal of the forest is mine,
> And the cattle on the thousand hills.
> I know every bird in the mountains,
> And the creatures of the field are mine.
> If I were hungry, I would not tell you,
> For the world is mine, and all this is in it.

When we grasp this revelation, the next step is surrender. We must surrender ownership of our possessions, surrender the illusion that we are in control and surrender our wills to the reality that it's all his.

God's Promise to the Tither

THOMAS WAS WONDERING, WHY would I want to do all this surrendering. Then he read the passage from Malachi 3:6–12 that reveals God's will towards a tither. It became truly clear to him that surrendering his will to God's will is advantageous and definitely produces a good character. Taking a closer look at this passage, it reveals five "I will" promises and a challenge from God. Beginning at Malachi 3:10, "Bring the tithes in full to the treasury, so that there is food in my house; put me to the test now like this, says Yahweh Sabaoth, and see if I do not open the floodgates of heaven for you and pour out an abundant blessing for you (singular)." (comment added) (NJB). Or in the New English Bible, "Bring the tithes into the treasury, all of them, let there be food in my house. Put me to the proof, says the Lord of Hosts, and see if I do not open the windows in the sky and pour a blessing on you as long as there is need." Within this verse are the first two "I will" promises and God's challenge.

    First, he says I will open the floodgates or windows of heaven to the tither. That is quite a powerful image! Thom closed his eyes and pictured looking over the Hoover Dam. He saw all that water being held back by the dam. Acres and acres of life-giving water are held in place by a single immoveable structure. Now, the floodgates to those dams are opened, fully opened. He felt the power, heard the thunder, and saw the force as megatons of water exploded from those flood gates! Now, he imagined that is the blessing God is releasing to him because of his tithe. A blessing in abundance that is his as long as there is a need! And this led straight into the second "I will" promise. God is releasing a blessing, singular. Imagine having a blessing that is like the power of water released from a floodgate. A single blessing! From his studies, Thomas knew there were examples all around him of this promise. Colonel Sanders, a tither, received a single blessing of being able to cook great chicken. He has been gone now for over 30 years and his blessing is still pouring forth. Ted Geisel, Dr. Seuss, had a blessing of being able to write children's stories. Next time he was in the library, he would look at all the various categories of books there are to choose from and remind himself that Dr. Seuss had a blessing. He considered Bill Gates. He was blessed with writing a single software program for IBM, the Disk Operating System, DOS. Look what became of that single blessing.

Thomas looked closely at this verse and saw the words "see if I do not" or "Put me to the proof." This is God's challenge to Thom regarding tithing. He is asking him to challenge his will on the subject of tithing. That is quite a powerful challenge. In contemporary language, he is "calling us out," drawing a line in the sand, asking him to try to prove his words and will false. Simply put he is saying, "I dare you to tithe and see if I don't give you what I said I would give you. Prove me a liar!" Tithing must be extremely important if God, the Supreme Commander of all Forces, the CEO of, well, of Everything, the Creator of Heaven and Earth, is willing to stake his reputation on it.

Thomas found the next two "I will" promises in Malachi 3:11. In the New English Bible translations, Thom read, "I will forbid pests to destroy the produce of your soil or make your vines barren (NEB)." In the Jerusalem Bible translations, he read, "For your sakes, I shall forbid the locust to destroy the produce of your soil or prevent the vine from bearing fruit in your field (NJB)." In this verse, the crops are representative of the blessing received from God. The pests or locust represents those forces that are preventing Thom from tithing and receiving God's "floodgate" blessing. Those forces could be internal and represent his own weakness and limitations such as, "I never seem to have enough money to tithe" (limitation-lack of budgeting education), or "I don't know where my money goes, all I know is that I never have enough" (weakness-impulse buying). Or they could be external and represent his enemies or even the Devil, such as "as soon as my credit cards are paid off, then I'll have enough to begin tithing" (enemies), or "when I can stop paying for my kids school activities, then I'll have the extra money to tithe" (Devil). Thomas remembered one of the benefits of tithing is that it teaches him to put God first and allow him to vanquish these pests. The fourth "I will" promise is centered on the concept of not letting his vines become barren. In other words, letting his blessing come to full fruition and not having premature delivery of it. In this "I will" God is promising the tither he will teach Thom how to hold onto his blessing and use it at the appropriate time.

The fifth "I will" promise is found in Malachi 3:12, "All nations shall count you happy, for yours shall be a favored land, (NEB)." "all the nations will call you blessed, for you will be a land of delights," (NJB). In this promise, God is saying he will favor and bless the tither. Thomas thought, what does it mean to be "favored"? He found synonyms for the word favor included chosen, esteem, preferential. Therefore, by tithing, God will give preferentially to Thomas. He will esteem him. He will include him has his chosen. Could this not also mean he is willing to view Thom as his "favored" son? To not only receive the preferential treatment of a favored child but also avoid punishment and have his mistakes overlooked. What a wonderful blessing to receive from tithing, to have God declare him as favored and to live his life in delight and happy!

The lesson Thomas was learning is by giving a little back to God, the tithe, he was building a good character, putting first things first, and being a partner in God's creation by being a giver. He was also learning is that if he could put God first with the tithe, he could begin to put himself second and start saving 10% for himself. As Proverbs 13:11 taught him:

> he who gathers money little by little, makes it grow.

REFLECTIONS

Thomas was feeling less like the rebellious teenager and was beginning to feel like he was transitioning into the wiser adult. He was becoming more fully conscious of God's grace and willing to become an obedient disciple. Don't get him wrong. He still had moments of rebellion, like wrapping his head around tithing. Mentally, he got it. Emotionally, it was a tricky thing to do.

He understood, and was beginning to feel, that through the Old Testament lessons he was learning. He was learning to become more obedient to God's Word. Learning to discipline himself to become more of a giver through the tithe. And feeling that through these lessons, he was building a good character for himself.

Thomas said to himself, "My vest is coming along nicely." God does have my back, even during those times I forget that he does. The back of my vest is the same. It's always there, even when I forget about it. The left front side of my vest, the Old Testament lessons, have taught me to be disciplined, to be a disciple. My vest is letting me be a faithful servant to God, letting me to begin to focus on higher things. It really is becoming a Uniform of the Steward."

Thom decided he would add a pocket to this side of the vest, the Old Testament piece of the pattern. It would remind him that the left hand should not know what the right hand is doing about his offerings. And to remember to give back a small portion, a tithe, to God to show his discipleship to be his steward

He continued his reflections on what he has learned so far. He was still full of wonder, amazement, and still had lots of questions. He was grace-filled for this stewardship journey God was leading him on. It was turning out to be much more of an adventure than he first planned for. And that was definitely okay with him.

Thom felt he was ready to begin cutting out the next piece of the pattern for his vest, his uniform of the steward. The front right side would be lessons he will learn from the New Testament. He was ready to move on from being a rebellious teenager to a wise adult. Ready to receive and practice the lessons of stewardship, the lesson of love.

PRAY

Lord, help me to be wise as I steward what you have given me and to be a risk taker when it comes to generosity. Amen.

New Testament Lessons

From Discipleship to Stewardship

How does one show their love, respect, fear of God in the New Testament? Thomas knew one answer was through the tithe. That was the beginning, it was not the end.

Abram brings the tithe to Melchizedek out of love not because of the Law or Commandments.

Jesus came to fulfill the Law with the new testament of love.

To begin this next part of his journey, Thom wanted to know more about how he would go from being a disciple to being a steward. He grasped that Jesus would be his guide, mentor, and example. How was Jesus going to guide, mentor and show him examples of this transition was where Thomas was stuck. So, as before, Thom began with what he knew.

He recalled the traditions of Jesus being born in a stable and lived about 33 years. Yet he changed the world. For many, he understood Jesus of Nazareth sparked a flame of hope and renewal and provided us lessons. That is when it clicked for Thom. Lessons! That's how Jesus is going to guide and mentor me. Through his lessons, his parables, his examples. Well, Duh! Saying to no one in particular, "You can be pretty dense sometimes Thom."

From this insight, Thomas asked what lessons did he already know, or think he knew, Jesus has taught him?

He knew Jesus gave people a vision larger than themselves. That's one of the reasons Thomas began this journey in the first place. He was looking to be something larger or better than what he was. Jesus often spoke about the significance of what his disciples were doing, and they could see and feel the long-lasting benefits of their work with him. They were changing people's lives for the good. Thomas could testify to the same feelings and see the changes both in his life and the lives of others as he became more of a disciple.

Jesus did the difficult things. Peter warned Jesus against going to Jerusalem. Jesus was aware of the danger and went anyway. He knew it was part of a larger plan. Thomas could definitely relate to this lesson! It was exceedingly difficult for Thomas to begin to discipline himself to following the old testament lessons. It still was hard. Because Thom was beginning to understand the larger vision, the difficulty of being a disciple was a little easier to bear and gave him courage to keep going.

Jesus refused to consider failure and was a turnaround specialist. He was able to take what the Pharisees, Romans, and others, threw at him and keep going. He tried to change for the better every situation he encountered. When he saw a need, he wasted no time in filling it. Often, he anticipated a need before others knew it and set himself on a path to meet that need. He came to give us a new mindset. One where we are each called to be a turnaround specialist. This lesson resonated with Thomas as he was seeing in his own life and was beginning to see other lives change as well because of the changes he was making to his own life.

Jesus looked for the best in others. He saw greatness in the most flawed of men and women. In Peter, though he denied him three times, three! Jesus said he was his rock. To Mary Magdalene he said, "Yes Mary, you've had men who weren't your husband. But you are capable of devoted love." Thom was so incredibly grateful for this lesson and got misty eyed when he thought about how Jesus saw in him what he, Thomas, could not see in himself. How appreciative Thom was for having begun this journey and how it has impacted his life and the ripple effect it was having on the lives he was touching.

Reflection: Are you ready to receive
your miracle of stewardship?

Jesus forgave. He saw mistakes as lessons. He gave hope and a spirit of peace to people overwhelmed by life. He said, "Come unto me all ye that labor and are heavy laden and I will give you rest." Oh my, oh my, how Thomas was thankful for recalling this lesson. He had made many a mistake and knew he would continue to make mistakes, a, er, correct that, he thought, learn a lesson. Yes, that sounded better. Thomas was looking forward to the day of rest.

Wow, as Thomas reflected back on all that he recalled there was a lot of lessons he had already gleaned without realizing it. That made him feel accomplished and motivated to learn more lessons from the new testament.

One idea that stuck him was that Jesus created an overflow from his giving, just like Malachi taught in a floodgate blessing. His stream of consciousness lead him to think about the cheerful giver and being joyfully obedient. Jesus defined joyful obedience primarily in terms of stewardship issues, this is, giving of one's life and resources. According to Jesus, to give joyfully in the manner of a good steward is to get in on life, it is life-giving. Thus, Jesus' frequent focus on issues related to money and possessions did not reflect an obsession. Rather, he simply recognized that money and possessions are a reflection of who a person is. Put another way, money and possessions represent distilled energy. Money takes intangible energy and turns it into something tangible. What we choose to do with our money and possession reflects our total sense of values. Seen in this light, money and possessions can never be an end in themselves; rather, they are simply a means for faithful service as a steward of God's goodness. Grace precedes giving. As grace-filled children of God, we respond to grace by recognizing that we have been entrusted with much. How we act out our stewardship is a reflection of our reception and awareness of grace from God. When we learn that there is joy in giving God also celebrates.

> Give, and it will be given to you; good measure, pressed down, shaken together, running over, will be put into your lap. For the measure you give will be the measure you get back.
> Luke 6:38

This made Thomas wonder, did Jesus ever carry money, did he have a coin purse? At the next bible study he would ask the associate minister her thoughts.

Well, Thom, that's an interesting question the associate minister said as bible study was just beginning. She gathered everyone's attention and relayed Thomas' question to the group. She said, "let's look at this question for today's study and see what the bible tells. Although the New Testament does tell us about Jesus and money, it does not reveal whether or not he carried any himself. We are told that Judas carried the moneybag for the group of disciples in John 12:5. So Jesus delegated that responsibility to others in the band that traveled with him, and they bought bread that was needed for themselves and Jesus."

"However, Jesus recognized the importance of money and the proper use of it. And he spoke of the principle may times. When the rich young ruler came to Jesus asking what he could do to inherit eternal life, Jesus told him to sell all he had, and the young man went away sorrowing as related to us in Luke 18:18–23. Jesus used this incident to state, "How hard it is for the rich to enter the kingdom of God. Indeed, it is easier for a camel to go through the eye of a needle than the rich to enter the kingdom of God.' Recall, those who heard this asked, 'Who then can be saved?' Jesus replied, 'What is impossible with men is possible with God (Luke 18:24–27).' It is possible with God for we know that a rich man named Joseph of Arimathea gave his tomb for Jesus to be laid in, look up Mathew 27:57."

"Jesus also gave a parable about the correct stewardship of money in Matthew 25:14–30. Two of the servants who received their master's talents were wise stewards, gaining more from what they had been given, and were thus rewarded. The one foolish servant who misused the master's talents, lost that talent and his reward. The principle is that all that we have belongs to the Lord and how we use it, as wise and good stewards, will determine rewards. These "talents" are inclusive of all of the details of our lives: time, money, relationships, and gifts. All we have is by the grace of God and being a wise servant who does all to the glory of God is our reasonable service as Romans 12:1 tells us."

"Jesus' teaching on the details of life, which includes money, was that God would provide for all of the believer's needs. 'But seek first his kingdom and his righteousness, and all these things will be given to you as well (Matt 6:33).' This truth is certainly illustrated by the widow's two mites in Mark 12:42. Whereas she gave to God all that she had, there were some rich who cast into the temple treasury from the abundance just for the show of it. The lesson that Jesus gave in all this was that the window gave more that all of the others. The implication here is that she gave her all to God and trusted him to supply her need."

"Thank you, Thom, for asking your question and giving us an opportunity to remember what Jesus and the New Testament teaches us about being discipled stewards."

LET'S START AT DISCIPLINE

Okay, Thomas was thinking to himself, I remember some of the big lessons Jesus taught in the New Testament, I've got it drilled into me that it all belongs to God, and I should be joyfully obedient through my tithe. But what about being disciplined in the New Testament, what is the lesson I should learn there?

Trusting in the lessons of prudence and knowledge he learned before, he let his bible fall open and see what it would reveal. It opened in the book of Hebrews and chapter 12 verses 3–11 is what first caught his eye.

> For consider him who endured such hostility from sinners against Himself, lest you become weary and discouraged in your

souls. You have not yet resisted to bloodshed, striving against sin. And you have forgotten the exhortation which speaks to you as to sons: "My son, do not despise the chastening of the LORD, Nor be discouraged when you are rebuked by him; For whom the LORD loves he chastens, And scourges every son whom he receives." If you endure chastening, God deals with you as with sons; for what son is there whom a father does not chasten? But if you are without chastening, of which all have become partakers, then you are illegitimate and not sons. Furthermore, we have had human fathers who corrected us, and we paid them respect. Shall we not much more readily be in subjection to the Father of spirits and live? For they indeed for a few days chastened us as seemed best to them, but he for our profit, that we may be partakers of his holiness. Now no chastening is joyful for the present, but painful; nevertheless, afterward it yields the peaceable fruit of righteousness to those who have been trained by it (NKJV).

All right, I get it, Thom was muttering to himself. Spare the rod, old testament lesson being reiterated in the New Testament. To be disciplined, especially to the tithe, is hard. A struggle -yes! If we genuinely want to call ourselves disciples and God wants to call us his sons, we must submit to his discipline. To quote Watchman Nee, "That strong self-assertive will of mine must go to the cross, and I must give myself over wholly to the Lord." As a tailor I cannot to make a vest if I do not give myself any cloth; and in just the same way I cannot expect God to live out his life in me if I do not give him my life in which to live. Without reservations, without controversy, I must give myself to him to do as he pleases with me.

Reinforcing this message, Thom found in Mark's gospel God's call to us to be disciples, (2:13-17) and being fruitful stewards (4:10-20).

What struck home was that Thom could no longer be irresponsible with God's possessions, confess his short-fallings as 1 John 1:9 taught him, trust in Jesus' forgiveness for his mistakes, er, lessons learn, and believe in the bigger vision Jesus was showing him.

Being discipline, a disciple, is the first step to being a steward. Check. It's also the first new lesson Thomas discovered from the New Testament.

WWJS—WHAT WOULD JESUS SAY

Following this thread of thought, what else did Jesus have to say about the old testament lessons within the new testament.

Thom began with Matthew 5:17-20 where Jesus says, "Do not think that I have come to abolish the Law or the Prophets; I have not come to abolish them but to fulfill them." Jesus goes on to give reasons to keep the Law and not break it or teach others to break it. Later on, in Matthew 6:33 Jesus states, "seek ye first the kingdom of God, and his righteousness, and all these things shall be added to you." In all of this Jesus is not inventing a new religion but recovering what he deemed to be the crux of the Old Testament witness. In keeping with his Hebrew scriptures, Jesus taught that joyful obedience is the fitting response to God's goodness and faithfulness, he affirmed that relationship with God is a matter both of deed and heart, and that no matter how low a person may sink, he or she still bears the potential for this kind of relationship with God and with others. As Jesus said earlier, he came to fulfill all that God has already given. Thus, the purpose of the first covenant from the old testament was to bring human beings to health and wholeness by restoring their created relationship with God. Jesus, as the agent of the new covenant, did not reject that purpose; he filled it full of meaning and vitality.

A fun fact that Thomas was learning was that Jesus said more about money than about any other subject, including prayer. In the Gospels, one verse in six focuses on material possessions. This made sense to Thom because he thought that Jesus, as a faithful Orthodox Jew would have learned and practiced tithing (how to be disciplined with handling material possessions). In fact, further along in Matthew, Jesus castigates scribes and Pharisees for an exaggerated externalism and absence of mercy but warns them not to neglect the tithe (Mt 23:28).

Thomas asked himself, if Jesus spent so much time talking about money, why didn't he teach about tithing? What Thom discovered in his studies was tithing was deeply ingrained in the fabric of the society in which Jesus ministered. There was no reason to preach about something the people were already doing. Thom also learned the first-century Christians tithed to the storehouses of the Lord, and in some cases, they sacrificed all that they had for the benefit of their brothers and sisters in Christ (Acts 4:34-37). The early Christians did not balk at the requirement to give. They rejoiced in the opportunity.

The lesson Thom was learning is that Jesus may not have taught about tithing, but he certainly taught that we are to give to the needy (Matthew 25:37-40), sacrificially (Mark 12:41-44), without a great public display or show (Matthew 6:1-4) and expect to receive in proportion to what we give (Luke 6:38) knowing that it is more blessed to give than to receive (Acts 20:35).

All of this was brought home for Thom when he read the parable of the tenants (Matthew 21:33-46) where the lesson is to give God his due or face the consequences. Which reinforced his early lessons learned from the old testament about regular giving and being a trustworthy steward and reiterated in I Corinthians 16:1–4 and 4:1–5.

Another thread Thom was picking up is within the discipline of giving is the principle of regularity. To give is to give regularly, preferably weekly, week in, week out. This takes giving out of the realm of mood. We don't give just when we feel like it, or just when our heartstrings have been plucked by some dramatic and sentimental appeal. We give when the time comes, regardless of our mood. Regularity takes a lot of the pain out of giving. Money is a part of our life. Money represents days and hours of sweat and tears. Money is a very part of us, and to part with it is a grief process. It's painful. A decision to give regularly takes a lot of that pain away. Regularity also saves us from self-deception. If we give nothing for a time, and then for a heartstring appeal we give a hundred dollars, we deceive ourselves that we are very generous. But if that's divided into two dollars a week, not many of us can claim great generosity from such a gift.

With those threads woven into his vest, he took a moment to pray, "Father, you are the most generous giver of all. Your giving isn't sporadic or hit-and-miss; you bless me all the time. Teach me to give as you give, with an open heart and open hands."

Thomas was beginning to see the larger vision. Going from being a disciple of the old testament lessons to being a steward of the new testament lessons means going from tithing as a discipline of love to giving on your honor out of love. Because we are not under the law, but under grace (Rom 6:14), God has put us on our honor. And when we think that God should do so much for us, how can we but honor Him? Thomas recalled the words of C.T. Studd, "If Jesus Christ be God and died for me, then no sacrifice can be too great for me to make for him." Then that tingly feeling ran all over Thomas as inspiration hit him. Jesus is lord over my finances, which gives him the absolute right to command me regarding my use of possessions and my attitude towards money (Matt 6:19–34). That I should be striving towards giving beyond the tithe (Matt 23:23) and I should be stewarding towards the Great Commission (Matt 28:18–20).

BEARING FIRST FRUITS . . . HOW?

It was a chilly Saturday morning and Thom had just finished his brisk walk around the park. It was a quick walk because not only was it brisk, but the wind was also biting, and Thom wanted to feel the warmth of the indoors. After fixing himself a cup of lemon ginger tea, he sat down at the kitchen table and began his devotions for the day. He was reading the Gospel of John when he came across how God appoints us to bear fruit, fruit that lasts (John 15:16). Still stuck in his old testament lessons, he thought tithing is the seed of this fruit. When we do the tithe, then God, in his love, gives us all that we ask. For God's love is not in getting but in giving. Giving in love just as Jesus commanded in John 15:12; to do all things in love.

Jesus wanted us to know that there is a better life than the life money could buy. It was available to all of us, and the cost could not be measured in dollars. Thom understood that Jesus wants us to have a full life. That life has to do with value. Part of a valued life is money, but not the most essential part. Truly rich is different than financially wealthy. Truly rich means that you have great relationships. Thomas was getting the picture that bearing fruit, fruit that last, help create relationship. Relationship with God, with friends, with community. Even those part of the global community you may not be related to. All because of the seed you plant.

So now what? Thomas thought. I planted the seed. How do I nurture it to grow and thrive so it can bear fruit? How do I adopt the mindset of a steward? The familiar parable of the talents (Matt 24:14-30 and Luke 19:12-27) came to mind as did the parable of the Unjust Steward (Luke 16:1-9). The people in these parables each did what naturally came to them. They relied upon their natural abilities. "Oh, now I get it." Thomas said out loud. "Natural abilities, as in their talents, that which was given to them according to their purpose." he was reminded of God's promise in Romans 8:28, "All things work together for the good of those who love God, to those who are called according to his purpose."

That's how you begin to nurture the seed. You use your "God given talent." Yep, Thomas thought, everything, as in everything, does come from God. Just like the Parable of the Talents (Thomas chuckled to himself at God's humor in the double meaning of the word talent) points out, all of the initial talents given are from the lord. He gave the talents freely to his servants and intended for them to use them and be blessed in the process. Reinforcing the messages of relationship and everything we have is a gift from God to us. God expects us to use what we have been given and, as we use it, to be blessed. God delights in people who give of themselves and who are willing to trust him to honor their efforts. Such people build a stronger relationship with God, give him joy, and they, in turn share that joy with others.

Thom thought it's unfortunate that many of God's people have buried their talent out of fear and received little or no increase just like the servant in the parable. Fear is one of the greatest enemies of faith. Thomas was thinking how he had faced his fears when he began this journey. How he had faced fear along the journey. And how he still was afraid as he continued his journey of discovering what stewardship really meant. He was more confident in facing his fear because of the improved relationship he had developed with God along this journey. How his relationship with his friends and church strengthened because of this journey, which gave him courage to face the fear. He knew part of facing that fear and being a good steward is doing the most with the talent, both ability and money, God has given him. Thom pondered, "if I believe that God is really going to bless me, what am I going to do about it? I need to invest in what I believe in. Everything in life is an investment. I need to invest in cloth, threads, and sewing machines for my business. I invest time and effort into relationships with my friends. I can't expect a fruitage where there has been no investment."

To nurture that seed you need to invest in it. It doesn't matter what the investment is, how large or small it is. Each labor, each task, each investment, each service of love nurtures the seed into a tree that bears fruit, fruit that last and build up the Body of Christ and moves it one more significant step forward towards fulfilling its mission and its service of the Lord and his kingdom.

The lessons Thomas was learning from the New Testament, especially about first fruits, was nowhere in the Gospels does Jesus hold forth a lower standard than that established in the Old Testament. He mentions the tithe only twice in Luke 11:42 and 18:12. We as Christians, become a form of first fruits to God through our redemption. To symbolize that position, Christians are to honor God through generous giving of their talents in both abilities and money. And those abilities come from God and take many varieties to form the Body of Christ (1 Cor 12). The New Testament standard is to give out of love as God has prospered each one (1 Cor 16:2).

Thomas realized that the questions he asked of himself, How do I nurture the seed to grow and thrive so it can bear fruit? How do I adopt the mindset of a steward? is answered throughout the New Testament with lessons found in the illustrations of the person who gave that donkey on which Jesus rode into Jerusalem on Palm Sunday, the woman who anointed Jesus's feet with her tears and wiped them with her hair, the folks who provided the upper room where Jesus and his disciples could observe Passover. All of them were called by the Lord and sent by the Lord to serve him right where they were in their daily occupations, and in their daily activities. They were called to serve the Lord in the marketplace, in the mainstream of their daily lives. They may not all have been full-time church workers, but they are all full-time Christians; and all are called to witness, to serve, to minister right there where they lived, worked, and played. All these Christians, and those like them, will be rewarded for their actions (Matt 19:27–30, 25:21, Heb 11:4, 13).

Thomas said to himself, "I'll also follow their examples of bearing first fruits. I'll serve the Lord out of love with my talents in my marketplaces and in the mainstream of my daily life. Then I too will receive the same reward to hear God say, 'Well done good and faithful servant.'"

Actions You Can Take

In your life experiences, what have you come to recognize as your foremost talents in each of these areas:

Spiritual gifts?

Physical abilities?

Mental capabilities?

Emotional temperament?

Material possessions?

NEW TESTAMENT STEWARDSHIP ATTRIBUTES

The realization Thomas had of bearing first fruits with his talents (both abilities and money) in his marketplaces and in the mainstream of his daily life got him to thinking, what are the other attributes of being a steward? He was learning that Christ often uses examples of worldly wealth to teach spiritual truths about his kingdom. So far Thom had found all but one reference to the kingdom of God began with a parable on money or possessions, and 16 of Christ's 38 parables dealt with these issues.

Galatians 5:22–26 taught him an effective steward will do everything out of love; love for God, love for others, love for the church, love for creation. A steward is willing to sacrifice time, talents, and money to address the emotional, spiritual, and physical needs of others. A supportive steward will find joy and gratitude both in receiving the abundant life that Christ came to give and in being a conduit of everything he or she has received. We will find joy in knowing that life has meaning that is imbued by the risen Christ and a sense that the kingdom is real and present in the here and now. One who is keeping in step with the Spirit will be a valuable steward of peace and creativity looking for a way to promote reconciliation and justice. A steward is patient and kind; to family, to friends, and to the person we meet in the mainstream of our daily life. A steward will be moved with compassion for those who need assistance and do whatever they can to help, while preserving the dignity and self-respect of others. The steward expresses faithfulness to the calling of God, whether that is in ministry, in marriage, in one's vocation or in steady support of the ministries one has committed to. A steward exhibits gentleness in dealing with others, communicating, and acting in a humble way to treat people with respect, as Jesus did. A steward learns self-control; resisting the temptation to consume more than one needs and learning instead to let go of needing the newest, latest, and greatest. A steward instead gets satisfaction in loving God, in giving, in engaging in healthy relationships and in living an authentic, contented, disciplined life.

From his Old testament lessons Thom remembered that God uses our finances to develop our character. He was learning Jesus uses parables regarding financial stewardship to teach us about the importance of developing Godly qualities such as perseverance, discipline, charity, compassion, sacrifice, integrity, and honesty. Money is an ideal training tool because God knows, "where your treasure is, there your heart will be also (Matt 6:21)." And Romans 6:16 declares we belong to what we give ourselves to. Through teaching us financial stewardship the Lord is preparing us for the day of eternal accounting where we will discover that,

> "Whoever can be trusted with very little can also be trusted with much, and whoever is dishonest with very little will also be dishonest with much. So if you have not been trustworthy in handling worldly wealth, who will trust you with true riches? And if you have not been trustworthy with someone else's property, who will give you property of your own (Luke 16:10–12)?"

Thomas noticed the conditional statement that is attached to faithfulness with money. It says, "If you cannot be faithful with money, why would you expect spiritual blessing from the Father?"

Thomas grasped the eternal stakes are so high that it becomes our duty to learn all that we can about stewardship. That we are born as stewards with resources lent to us by God, The challenge is to follow Christ's example of servant-stewardship, recognizing our lack of rights from the beginning, just like it says in 1 Timothy 6:7, "For we brought nothing into this world, and we can take nothing out of it." Stewardship is God's way of raising people, not man's way of raising money.

> My money is not my money. It is a resource God has gifted to me.

That was the crux of it Thom was thinking. Money. Is it used for lust of flesh, lust of the eye, pride of life; or used to promote reconciliation and justice, helping those who need assistance, or in steady support of the ministries one has committed to. It's both and it's neither. Money can do both because all it is, is a tool. A tool to teach us stewardship. Or a tool to temporarily satisfy our lust and pride. Jesus knows our relationship with the Lord is shaped by what we think about throughout each day. If our thoughts primarily deal with money and worry over debt, our focus will separate us from God. We become undisciplined, we become fearful.

In reading about debt in the New Testament, Thomas found Romans 13:8, "Let no debt remain outstanding, expect the continuing debt to love one another, for he who loves his fellow man has fulfilled the law." Diving deeper into this verse Thom found that the Greek word for debt means obligation or to owe someone something. He considered that as long as we are meeting our obligations, and as long as the debt is being serviced according to the contract, the debt is acceptable. That scripture does not prohibit borrowing, nor does it encourage it. God does not want his people to be in debt, the only thing we are to owe others is our love, which we are to give freely and in tangible forms. We are to be givers, not borrowers.

One of Satan's greatest spiritual weapon is fear. One of his greatest natural weapons is debt. Debt lures and tempts, consumes, and crushes. It not only separates us from the money the Lord has entrusted to us but can also separate us from relationships. "A man is slave to whatever has mastered him." (2 Pet 2:19) came to Thomas' mind. Much of the time greed is the handmaiden to debt. Luke 12:15 says, "Be on your guard against all kinds of greed; a man's life does not consist in the abundance of his possessions." Greed is about taking unscrupulous advantage of another person because of the fear of lack of abundance. People fear life is passing them, they don't have enough. Others fear the future will be disastrous. They feel they must hoard their money or get the absolute maximum dollar out of every investment. Money itself ensnared them. When we fall to these kinds of fears, money creates a hold on us, usually at the expense of our relationships, including our relationship with God. Thomas found a great verse in the Bible that puts it very succinctly, "Perfect love drives out fear (1 John 4:18)." Put the verse in reverse, "Perfect fear drives out love." From that Thom concluded that the opposite of fear is love. Fear drives a wedge into our relationships and that fear comes through finances in particular. Fear causes failure. Jesus in his parable of the talents punished the unprofitable servant not for failing to succeed, but for failing to try.

The fear of trying shouldn't lead us to become financial drifters whose financial planning consists merely of balancing our checkbook and the end of the month. This would be like building our financial homes on the sand (Matt 7:26–27) and will have a detrimental effect on our stewardship and spiritual maturity. Our plan should be we work, "in order that he may have something to give to those in need (Eph 4:28)." The plan is to create little profit pockets from what we earn, become more generous, pay off debt, and never go back to being controlled by money. In other words, savings from goods and services are not channeled back into lust and pride but are used to build assets and relationships. As the Lord conforms to us the character of a godly steward, he will always ask us to separate from those things, like fear, that he knows are not good for us. He will ask us, guide us to follow his plan of being loving stewards. If we choose not to follow his plan, then we could face the consequences James warns us about in his letter to the twelve tribes scattered among the nations (Jas 3:2, 5–6, 8–10):

> We all stumble in many ways. If anyone is never at fault in what he says, he is a perfect man, able to keep his whole body in check. Likewise the tongue is a small part of the body, but it makes great boosts. Consider what a great forest is set on fire by a small spark. The tongue also is a fire, a world of evil among the parts of the body. It corrupts the whole person, sets the course of his life on fire, and is itself set on fire by hell. But no man can tame the tongue. It is a restless evil, full of deadly poison. With the tongue we praise our Lord and Father, and with it we curse men, who have been made in God's likeness. Out of the same mouth come praise and cursing. My brothers, this should not be.

The lesson Thomas was learning is that Jesus is telling us to use it or lose. Money is worth something now, but it won't be for long. Use all the resources at your disposal to reduce financial debts to debts of gratitude. That's what the Unjust Steward did, and that's what he's commended for. There are many things money can't buy, but there are some things of eternal significance that money can buy. Money can buy Bibles and Sunday School materials, money can support missionaries, pastors, and evangelists, money can feed and clothe the poor, money can fund a block party and build bridges between neighbors, money can encourage someone who thinks God has forgotten him. A wise investment of God's recourse is when we put it towards things that help others to know and love Christ.

That's the point, Thom believed, use God's money to win kingdom friends.

It had been a fruitful day for Thomas. As he got ready for bed, he mentally ran through a list of attributes of a steward. They included:

- A steward is giving.
- Address the needs of others while preserving their dignity and self-respect.
- Promotes reconciliation and justice.
- Faithfull to God's calling.
- Self-controlled, resisting temptation and fear.
- Living debt free (Rom 13:8–10).
- Christ's lordship and ownership of all things (Rom 10:5–13).
- Stewarding our individual gifts (Rom 12:4–8).

And the top attribute is: Do everything out of love. As Thomas drifted off to sleep, he said this prayer:

Holy Spirit, thank you for coming into my heart and gifting me with power, love, and self-control. Thank you for the unique gifts you have given me. Dwell in me and lead me every day. Teach me so that I will grow in maturity as a steward of those gifts and of the corner of the kingdom in which you have planted me. Amen.

THE NATURE OF A SERVANT

It was another Hump Day, and it was also Bible Study night. Of course, Thomas was well prepared and ready to participate and contribute to the study group—not! It was a busy week so far for Thomas and he hadn't done a thing to prepare for Bible Study. Before leaving work, he went to his church's website, found his Bible study's page, and looked up the topic for tonight's study. The topic was, "The nature of a servant." Well, that was convenient, considering that topic sort of fits in with his overall stewardship journey. They were going to start with Luke 12:48 and wander around the New Testament from there to get a picture of servant-stewardship. While commuting home Thomas looked up Luke 12:48 on his smartphone. "From everyone who has been given much, much will be demanded; and from the one who has been entrusted with much, much more will be asked." This verse reminded Thom of the verse in Philippians he read this morning during his devotions. Where Paul says that those who follow Jesus are to imitate him by giving up their rights; by taking on the very nature of a servant (Phil 2:7). Wow, Thom thought, the Christian steward is called to live in courageous faith to take on the nature of a servant. He recalled all those stories his parents told about being stewards/servers/servants and the demands the public had upon them. It was hard, exhausting work!

During the study they read 1 Timothy 6:17–19 which says:

> Instruct those who are rich in this present world not to be conceited or to fix their hope on the uncertainty of riches, but on God, who richly supplies us with all things to enjoy. Instruct them to do good, to be rich in good works, to be generous and ready to share, storing up for themselves the treasure of a good foundation for the future, so that they may take hold of that which is life indeed.

The associate pastor said that this passage is not a recommendation. It is a command that as seen in verses 17 and 18. She went on to say that it is a command for two reasons. "One, God is the source of our hope. Our source of hope is not wealth, but God who gives the wealth. This thinking replaces our arrogance with humility. Two, God gives wealth for a purpose. God does not want us to simply spend on ourselves. We are to be willing to share. This thinking replaces our selfishness with generosity."

This lead to a conversation about how do you know if you are serving God or yourself with the wealth he provides. The associate pastor suggested "one measure of determining which master you serve is whether you worry about riches. In Matthew 6:25–34, Christ said we shouldn't worry about life and whether we will have food to eat or clothes to wear. When we begin worrying about these things, we soon find ourselves serving riches rather than God." She went on to say, "Christ is calling us to serve God rather than our worldly riches. Live by faith, trusting God to provide for your needs. Be generous, tithe on your income whether you can afford to or not. Live within your means, don't use credit to acquire a higher lifestyle that God intended for you. Rise each day excited to serve the Lord rather than your wallet. Be content with the life God has given you, and you will find a happiness that money can't buy."

She pointed the study group to Corinthians, chapter 11, were the Christians in Corinth were living for themselves by overeating and overdrinking at the expense of the poorer members of the community. She said, "This is crucial text about stewardship of material possessions. If we are not sharing our resources with poorer believers, we must be cautious against taking the Lord's Supper in an unworthy manner." She went on, "We are called upon very clearly in the Bible to take care of the poor and to provide for the poor, but the poor are always assumed in the Scriptures to be those who are not capable of taking care of themselves. The poor are nearly always defined as widows and orphans; those who do not have a designated provider with a family structure. The 'poor' in the Bible is a classification according to a lack of a provider, we are to help those who have nobody else to help them. Look at John 12:8, 'You will always have the poor among you.' There is no blessing attached with poverty, in this verse or any other verse. Jesus was pointing out to his disciples the reality of humankind as a whole, not God's desire for humankind. He was stating what is, not what God wishes."

The associate pastor, Sarah, brought the study to a close by giving everyone homework for next time they meet. Sarah asked us to look at 2 Corinthians 8–9 where Paul provides the longest sustained writing on giving in the New Testament; he address motives, priorities, and principles for Christian giving as he instructs the Corinthians about participation in his collection for the poor. She hinted to pay particular attention to the grace of giving in 8:1–7, accountability in finances and other areas (8:16–24) and a heart for giving (9:6–15). If you want to know the true nature of a servant, these two chapters give you the blueprint.

When Thomas got home and was winding down for the evening, there was something about tonight's Bible Study that was nagging him. Like a piece of a pattern that needed to be placed in its proper position. Then it stuck him, "Ah, my vest pocket!" But when you give alms, do not let your left hand know what your right hand is doing, that your alms may be in secret; and your Father who sees in secret will repay you (Mt 6:3–4). Then Thom has the thought of we do not sin when others know we give. We sin when we want them to know that we give. There's that lesson again of giving out of love and not out of selfishness or being a show-off. God is not impressed when we give to get. God blesses giving that is motivated to help others like Ephesians 6:28 says and glorify him as in Colossians 3:17. Part of the nature of a servant is in the giving out of love.

Pray

Lord, I want to be a good steward of this earth. Show me your will regarding how I should think, pray, and act. Amen.

From Giving as Obedience to Giving as Love

GIVING AS OBEDIENCE

During his commute to work the next day, Thomas was ruminating over last night's Bible Study discussion. From his Old Testament studies he understood the first task of stewardship is obedience. He recalled from his studies a quote he ran across from theologian A. W. Tozer that says:

> If we are alert enough to hear God's voice, we must not content ourselves with merely 'believing' it. How can any man believe a command? Commands are to be obeyed, and until we have obeyed them, we have done exactly nothing at all about them. And to have heard them and not obeyed them is infinitely worse than never to have heard them at all, especially in the light of Christ's soon return and the judgment to come.

Thom had book marked some passages on obedience. Ecclesiastes sums up the whole duty of man (Ecclesiastes 12:13–14), John 14:6–21 reinforces the thought, and 1 John 2 and 3 brings it home.

These ruminations snapped a connection into place for Thom. The difference between productivity, being a good steward with what God has put you in charge of, and lack of productivity is the difference between obeying the Word and not obeying the Word. God measures productivity according to our ability to obey the Word of God. Humanity was actually created to receive instructions from God internally through the Holy Spirit. When we allow the Spirit to lead us, we can begin to step into the realm of productivity. So, to be a successful steward, you must obey God's Word.

This reminded Thom of St. Paul's perspective of New Testament obedience he wrote about in Romans 6:15-19. That little exploration would have to wait, as he was pulling into the parking lot for work.

After loading the dishwasher that night, Thomas recalled The Romans' verses he thought about earlier that morning. If, according to Paul, we look at obedience as a slave metaphor, when we are a slave to earthly riches, we are not only depriving God of glory, others of help, and ourselves of reward, but to destine ourselves to perpetual insecurity; the more we have the more we have to worry about. The old adage, where your treasure is, there your heart is also, (Matt 6:21) came to mind. That lead to the thought about those that say, "I don't tithe, or can't tithe, because it's too hard, or I can't afford it. Are really already tithing. All they have to do to see what they're tithing about, what they are putting first in their lives, is look at their expenses and see where their resources are going. That will show what they are tithing about.

This led Thomas to think about the verses that come before it, "Don't store up for yourselves treasures on earth, but store up for yourselves treasures in heaven. "(Matt 6:19-20) he noticed that the verses do not say it's wrong to store money, or to have concerns for personal finances. Jesus not even saying it's wrong to desire treasures, to desire great wealth. He says store up for yourselves treasures. Store it up in heaven, Jesus says. In heaven, not on earth, not on earth but in heaven; just in heaven. Why? There are three primary reasons why. First is safety. Jesus says treasure on earth is susceptible to corruption, decay, and theft. The second reason is yield. Treasure in heaven is high yield. Here in this world we like to invest money to get 5, 8, or 10 percent return. Scripture talks about heavenly investments yielding 30, 60 or hundredfold return. That's 3,000, 6,000, or 10,000 percent! Third is a wellness issue associated with the storehouse of heaven. Verse 21 says, Where your treasure is, there your heart will be also." Your money is going to follow your heart, no doubt. A new car, bigger house, vacation paid for with credit. But there's a reciprocal reaction. Your money goes that direction, stored in heaven, and then your heart goes all the more toward that thing.

Once again Thomas was realizing the lessons being taught to him through the New Testament. To obey is to follow the Word. To follow the Word is to store up our treasures in heaven. This helps us to be better stewards by sharing our treasures and learning the lessons found in Luke 12:15, Acts, 2:42-47 and 2 Corinthians 9:6-8.

If you're not obeying God, why should he listen to you?

Thomas' evening devotional verses were John 16:23-42. In reading these verses, Thomas asked the Father to help him be a better steward, to be a tither so he could advance God's Kingdom, to demonstrate love to him and his mom and dad to provide shelter, food, clothing, secure a foundation and future, create opportunities, and enjoy life. And to give love to his neighbors and help the needy so that his joy may be complete.

As he went to bed, he prayed, "God and loving Father, help me to obey you with all of my heart, soul, and mind. Amen."

GIVING AS WORSHIP

The seasons were changing, and Christmas would soon be here. Plus, it was payday, and Thomas was thinking about what presents we would be purchasing for friends and family. This reminded him of the first Christmas presents from the wise men. Since it had been a few months since he had done any research for his stewardship journey, Thom thought we would poke around a bit regarding the story of the three wise men.

Being a couch potato on a Saturday, Thomas was surfing the web about the story of the three wise men. He found out some interesting things, like there were probably were more the three of them. Three gifts, yes, three wise men, maybe not. He also learned that the contingent of wise men came a little later than at the actual birth of Jesus. Next, he learned that the sequence of the visit was very important. When the wise men finally arrived to see the young child Jesus in Mary and Joseph's house the first thing they did was worship him. Then they gave him their gifts. Worship first, offerings second. That piqued Thomas' curiosity. In Matthew 2:11 it says they "open their treasures." Why would they do this Thom thought. What he discovered was that the gifts of the wise men "opened up the windows of heaven." Goosebumps ran down Thomas' arms. The gifts to the tither from Malachi. Oh, this was getting very interesting. This "opening up the windows of heaven" gave God the right to empower the ministry of Jesus the Christ. These gifts/money represented a natural seed into the ministry of Jesus that releases the spiritual blessings of God into his life and into the lives of the wise men. The spiritual power unleashed by the wisemen's gifts continues to pay dividends today as we are beneficiaries of the ministry of Jesus the Christ. The wise men did not drop the money/gifts in the offering plate; they sowed it into his life.

For Thomas, what this meant was the purpose of giving is to unleash the awesome power of the Spirit of God in his life and others. God is trying to show us the spiritual principal of sowing and reaping. When we give God our best, he is obligated to give us his best.

As Thom continued surfing, he came across Luke 6:38:

> Give, and it shall be given unto you; good measure, pressed down, and shaken together, and running over, shall men give into your bosom. For with the same measure that ye mete withal it shall be measured to you again.

Thomas was beginning to see a connection, or learn a lesson, between what he learned about "where your treasure is" and obeying the Word. We lose sight of "windows of heaven" and focus on making money for the sole purpose of participating in that which we see and like. We offer our talents, abilities, and efforts to collect a paycheck that will allow us to claim pieces of the earth. The earth subtly becomes the object of our affection, our treasure. What the Word describes is the spirit of man as the candle or light of the Lord (Proverbs 20:27). The Spirit provides insight. Paul tells us in Galatians 6:17 the flesh (Pitfalls of Shoddy Stewardship) is contrary to the Spirit (Prudence, Prosperity & Knowledge). Jesus came to reestablish a spiritual connection between God and humankind (to open the blind eyes). In the book of John, Thomas discovered, Jesus asserts that the time has come for true worshippers to worship God in spirit and in truth. Thom understood there are many ways to worship, and for him he summed it up like this: respect the authority of the Spirit of God. Worship is about reverence and obedience. Worship implies a proper relationship with God.

Just like the relationship the first century Christians had with God. As Thom was learning on the internet and through the book of Acts, believers over and over again sold their possessions, put their money in the ministry, and took freely from the pot as they had need (Acts 2:45, 4:35). In other words, they gave 100 percent, fully expecting to be taken care of by the work of the ministry. Their focus was on the ministry, not the money. The money issue is a matter of focus, focus comes from the eyes. God holds the vision. The earth is merely a resource in the vision. Since folks keep treating the earth as the actual vision, people remain confused and unfilled. If your vision only revolves around figuring out how to obtain as much of the stuff you see around you as fast as humanly possible, you will miss the plan and purpose of God. Again Matthew 6:19–21 came to mind for Thomas.

As Thomas was putting all his thought together involving what he was learning, he grasped the act of worship came first for the wise men, then they gave their offerings as part of their worship. And what about now, does that still hold true today? Thom assumed a lot of people seem to think the reason we have an offering during Sunday services is because the church needs to pay its bills and also wants to do good things with the money that is collected. The church does need to pay its bills, and it probably does good things with the money put in the offering plate, but that is not why there is an offering during the Sunday service.

According to Mark Allan Powell, the offering is an act of worship, an instance in which we are invited to give up something that we value, our money (which is really his in the first place), as a sacrifice to God. In many ways, it is the high point of liturgy. We come to church to worship God and at no other point in the service are we provided with so pure an opportunity for worship as this.

We are invited to put money in the offering-plate on Sunday not because the church needs our money, but because we want and need to give it. We have a spiritual need to worship God, and through our offering we are able to express our love and devotion for God in a way that is simple and sincere. The motivation of the giver is what counts most, not the size of the gift or the degree of benefit to the recipient as Mark 12:42-44 show us. The good news of stewardship is that church offerings are not fund-raising rituals but acts of worship in which we are invited to express our heartfelt devotion to God who is so good to us.

As Thom was winding down his studies on the internet, he read in Hebrews 7:1-22 giving as worship which reinforced his lessons on the matter. As he closed his laptop he prayed, "God, thank you for your good gifts to me, for giving me everything I need. I pray that I will worship you fully by giving back to you with a joyful and loving heart.

GIVING AS HABIT

As Thomas was progressing on his stewardship journey, he was intrigued by what Apostle Paul wrote in his letter about the potential benefits the habit of giving has for everyone involved. What Thom found is that Paul urged his readers to make giving a natural and regular part of their Christian walk. He saw it as a way for believers to care for each other and to stay unified in purpose. Not only that, but Paul also understood the importance the habit of righteous giving has on a Christian's future. The teachings of Jesus, like the one the one found in Luke 12:32-34, were never far from Paul's thoughts. Paul lifted up Jesus' life and teaching as the example we should follow for giving, as he wrote in 2 Corinthians 8:9, "For you know the grace of our Lord Jesus Christ, that though he was rich, yet for your sake he become poor, so that you through his poverty might become rich." The Apostle hoped that by seeing Jesus as the model for the habit of giving, believers would feel inspired to look at giving not as a burden, but as an opportunity to become more Christlike. What Thomas was learning is that Paul's letters modeled what it looks like to live to give.

As Thomas studied Paul's writings more in depth, there were five lessons he was learning: 1. God's blessings equip us to give to others. 2. The act of giving is more important that the amount. 3. Having the right attitude about giving matters to God. 4. The habit of giving changes us for the better, and 5. Giving should be an ongoing activity.

God's Blessing Equips Us to Give to Others

From his passed lessons Thomas recalled that we are meant to be streams of blessing, not reservoirs. To be better givers it helps to remember how much we already have. Paul's desire was for us to lift up thanks to God, then ask him if there's anything he wants us to pass forward. Doing that helps meet a need and keeps us from holding onto our possessions too tightly. Thomas found that this is reinforced in Paul's letter to the Corinthians and his letter to Timothy:

> God is able to bless you abundantly, so that in all things at all times, having all that you need you will abound in every excellent work (2 Cor 9:8).

> Now he who supplies seed to the Sower and bread for food will also supply and increase your store of seed and will enlarge the harvest of your righteousness. You will be enriched in every way so that you can be generous on every occasion and through us your generosity will result in thanksgiving to God (1 Cor 9:10–11).

> Command those who are rich in this present world not to be arrogant nor to put their hope in wealth, which is so uncertain but to put their hope in God, who richly provides us with everything for our enjoyment, command them to do good, be rich in honorable deeds and to be generous and willing to share (1 Tim 6:17–18).

The Act of Giving is More Important Than the Amount

Jesus commended the poor window who gave a small offering to the church treasury because she gave out of what little she had. Paul asks us to let regular giving become one our holy habits, whatever circumstances we find ourselves in. The important thing is to decide to do what we can when we can. Then we can watch how God multiplies our gift as Thom found in these passages:

> In the midst of a very severs trial, their overflowing joy and their extreme poverty welled up in rich generosity. For I testify that they gave as much as they were able and even beyond their ability (2 Cor 8:2–3).
>
> On the first day of every week each one of you should set aside a sum of money in keeping with your income, saving it up, so that when I come no collection will have to be made (1 Cor 16:2).
>
> For if the willingness is there, the gift is acceptable according to what one has, not according to what one does not have (2 Cor 8:12).

Having the Right Attitude About Giving Matters to God

Paul felt joyful about offering his whole life to serve others physically and spiritually and reminds us that tithing should come out of a humble and hopeful heart. Our tributes need to be driven not by guilt, attention-seeking, or any other reason but a sincere desire to show God's mercy. This was reinforced for Thomas when he read these verses:

> Each of you should give what you have decided in your heart to give, not reluctantly or under compulsion, for God loves a cheerful giver (2 Cor 9:7)
>
> If it is giving, then give generously (Rom 12:8)
>
> If I give all I possess to the poor and give over my body to hardship that I may boast, but do not have love, I gain nothing (1 Cor 13:3)

The Habit of Giving Changes Us for the Better

Paul had seen the transforming effect tithing had on believers who made giving a priority. As we sincerely give to his causes, God will do a wonderful work within our hearts while he ministers around us.

We will become more God-centered as witnessed in Acts 20:35, "in everything I did, I showed you that by this kind of demanding work we must help the weak, remembering the words the Lord Jesus himself said: 'it is blessed to give than to receive.'"

We will continue to grow in empathy and mercy as Paul wrote in 2 Corinthians 8:7, "But just as you excel in everything-in faith, in speech, in knowledge, in complete earnestness and your love for us-see that you also excel in this grace of giving."

We will gain contentment with what we have as Paul told Timothy, "For the love of money is a root of all kinds of evil. Some people, eager for money, have wandered from the faith and pierced themselves with many griefs.

Giving Should Be an Ongoing Activity

The last lesson Thom was learning, and one that he was beginning to practice with more regularity, is that with time, giving can become a lifestyle for individuals and congregations. Paul tried to keep his young churches strong in this vital work by acknowledging, encouraging, and challenging them.

> Last year you were the first not only to give but also to have the desire to do so. Now, finish the work, so that you're eager willingness to do may be matched by completion of it (2 Cor 8:10–11).

> Let us not become weary in doing good, for ask the proper time we will reap a harvest if we do not give up. Therefore, as we have opportunity, let us do good to all people, especially to those who belong to the family of believers (Gal 6:9–10).

> We should continue to remember the poor, the very thing I had been eager to do all along (Gal 2:10).

> Share with the Lord's people who are in need. Practice hospitality (Rom 12:13).

Thomas thought that with prayer and continued study, God will help him to persevere through any fatigue or discouragement until giving is a source of joy, whether or not he sees the results.

That Sunday as Thomas was attending church, he saw the sermon was titled, "New Testament Principles of Giving: Ten Ways to Give That Please God." he thought, this must be the week for numbered lists. First it was the five lessons he learned from studying the writings of Apostle Paul. Now the pastor was giving him another list. What are the odds of that happening? Then he chuckled as he realized that with God's math, the odds are always favorable.

The pastor began, "Good morning, beloved in Christ. We gather today as a community of grace, knowing that wherever two or more are gathered in his name, God is with us. Let us take a moment to breathe in this sacred space and be still, as we prepare our hearts to hear God's word."

He continued, "The churches in Macedonia, the northern province of Greece, had given to a collection for poor saints in Jerusalem. In 1 Corinthians 16, and in 2 Corinthians 8 and 9, the Apostle Paul used their examples to inspire the believers at Corinth to give. These three texts provide some of the richest teaching on giving in the New Testament. Within them we will find ten ways to give that please God.

The first is God is pleased when you give even though you are overwhelmed with problems. 2 Corinthians 8:1-2 reads, 'Now, brethren, we wish to make know to you the grace of God which has been given in the churches of Macedonia, that in a great ordeal of affliction their abundance of joy and their deep poverty overflowed in the wealth of their liberality.' The Macedonians gave even though they were being ridiculed, robbed, beaten, and imprisoned for their faith. How should we apply this to our lives? We should give to God even when we are overwhelmed with problems.

Second, God is pleased when you give even though you are in poverty. As we read in 2 Corinthians 8:2, In a great ordeal of affliction their abundance of joy and their deep poverty overflowed in the wealth of their liberality.' Even though the Macedonian Christians were in deep poverty, they gave to God's work. For us, no matter how bad our financial condition, we can still give something to God. And he expects us to.

Third, God is pleased when you give beyond your ability. In the third verse of second Corinthians it says, 'For I testify that according to their ability and beyond their ability they gave of their own accord.' The Macedonians gave what they could afford to give and what they could not afford to give! They gave more than seemed humanly reasonable. God is pleased when we give sacrificially. When I was a younger pastor, I responded to people who told me they were not able to give by saying, Great! Then you can give. If you're not able to give, then you can give! You can give even if you can't give-beyond your ability!

Forth, God is pleased when you give generously. Recall in second Corinthians 8:2 the Macedonians gave generously, even though they were in abject poverty. God wants us to give liberal amounts with generous hearts to his work.

The fifth way we please God is when we give eagerly. Begging us with much entreaty for the favor of participation in the support of the saints (2 Cor 8:4). These harassed, poor believers actually begged and pleaded with Paul to let them have the privilege of sharing in the financial ministry to the

Jerusalem Christians. God wants us to be eager to give. For us, this means the offering should be the highlights of our worship each week!

The sixth way God is pleased is when you give cheerfully. Read second Corinthians chapter nine, verse seven. 'Let each one do just as he has purposed in his heart; not grudgingly or under compulsion, for God loves a cheerful giver.' God doesn't want us to give out of sense of pressure or guilt, but with joy. Please note that this does not mean we can wait to give until we feel like it! In many cases we must start giving before we start feeling the joy. It also does not mean that the pastor should not challenge people to give. There is a dramatic difference between challenging people to give and using guilt manipulation to compel them to give. The former is our responsibility; the latter is sin.

Seventh, God is pleased when you give yourself to him and to your spiritual leaders along with your money. Look at 2 Corinthians 8:5. The Macedonians were devoted to the Lord, to Paul, and to their other spiritual leaders. Once we have given ourselves to the Lord and to his appointed spiritual leaders, the giving follows naturally. The priority of devotion revealed in this verse is critical. Increased giving will flow from devotion to Christ, first, and loving respect for church leaders, second. Poor giving is often due to lack of devotion to Christ, and lack of trust in, or respect for, a church's spiritual leaders.

The eighth way our giving pleases God is when you accept your personal responsibility to give. First Corinthians chapter 16, verse two says, 'On the first day of every week let each one of you put aside and save, as he may prosper, that no collection be made when I come.' God expects each one of us to give-no exceptions, no excuses.

Ninthly, God is pleased when you carefully plan your giving. Paul commanded the Corinthians to set aside and save money every Sunday in anticipation of his arrival to collect the money. He didn't want a last-minute rush to find some spare change to put in the collection plate. God wants us to carefully plan our giving to his work. This involves choosing a time to give, like each pay period, or once a month, a form of giving, such as cash, check, automatic payments, a place to give like here at this church, and an amount to give.

And finally, the tenth way to please God with our giving is when you base your giving on the level of your prosperity. A basic guideline in deciding how much to give is to do so in proportion to the level of our financial prosperity. The more we get, the more we should give to God. The greater the income, the higher the percentage of it we should give away. But how do we choose a percentage? I'm convinced that in order to fulfill these New Testament principles of giving, Christians in every culture, and in every social-economic condition, around the world today should start by giving a minimum of 10% of their income to the Lord. Remember, God owns all our money and possessions, and it is he who 'richly supplies us with all things to enjoy (1 Tim 6:17). It is God's money, not ours, which we are deciding on a percentage to give from. Does it seem reasonable to give a mere 1–3% of our income to the God who gave it all to us in the beginning? Let's please God with our giving-amen!"

Well, Thom was thinking as he was heading home from church, that was fascinating. Most of what pastor said supported what he found from his Old Testament disciplines and with his New Testament lessons. It was still hard to hear some of it. That rebellious teenager still learning, Thomas supposed. Overall, he was glad that what he was learning and had learned aligned with what pastor was preaching. He was disciplining himself to give and striving to reach that 10% mark. Even though it didn't feel joyful all the time. He understood, with time it would get easier, was getting easier and had joyful moments.

GIVING AS LOVE

Pastor mentioned, in his tenth point of his sermon, that he thought giving should start at 10%. In other words, the tithe. Thomas understood that part from his Old Testament studies. What Thom wondered was how often is the tithe mentioned in the New Testament. What he discovered was that the tithe is mentioned a scant three times in the New Testament. In Matthew 23:23, which also is paralleled in Luke 11:42, Luke 18:12 and Hebrews 7:5–9. When Thomas looked at the context in which it is referenced in these passages, he found that tithing is not the definitive standard of giving for the Christian who is living and walking in the footsteps of love embodied. What linked these verses together for him was that we are the stewards of everything God had conferred on us by which we are able to help our neighbors and are required to render account of our stewardship. Moreover, the only right stewardship is that which is tested by the rule of love.

All this reminded and reinforced the lessons he learned from Apostle Paul. Paul taught that giving was to voluntary. The believers were to give willingly and freely as a response of love to Christ. Paul indicated that willing and voluntary giving is proof of the sincerity of our love for God and other believers. According to him, Jesus was the perfect example of the spirit about which he was speaking. He willingly and voluntarily gave his life out of love for the lost that they, being poor, might become rich in Christ.

As believers we are to determine what God wants us to give, willingly, freely, and voluntarily from a heart of love; commit to that; follow through and give what God has laid on our heart.

Thomas reread verse 12 of 2 Corinthians chapter eight to confirm that our giving should be done according to how God has prospered us. The New Testament lesson Thomas was learning is God does not set a specific amount that each believer is to give. What he expects is that each believer will evaluate what she has and what she needs, as well as what others have and need in an open and honest manner. Then, before God and by the Spirit's leading, the believer is to decide what she can, and is willing to give, and do so. Paul says this even more plainly in 2 Corinthians 9:7, "Each man should give what he has decided in his heart to give, not reluctantly or under compulsion, for God loves a cheerful giver."

What occurred to Thom was that every time you do that your life touches another with the love and the grace and the gospel God had given to you. You are showing the fruit of the Spirit, which is love, joy, peace, patience, kindness, goodness, faithfulness, gentleness, and self-control (Gal 5:22).

He wondered what else the fruit of the Spirit looks like in an effective steward. What he found was that an effective steward will, above all, do everything out of love; love for God, love for others, love for the church, love for creation. She will be willing to sacrifice time, talents, and treasures to address the emotional, spiritual, and physical needs of others. She will find joy and gratitude both in receiving the abundant life that Christ came to give and in being a conduit of everything she had received. An effective steward finds joy in knowing that life has meaning that is imbued by the risen Christ, and a sense that the kingdom is real and present in the here and now. One who is keeping in step with the Spirit will be an effective steward of peace, creatively looking for ways to promote reconciliation and justice. An effective steward will be patient and kind; to family, to friends, to the clerk in the store and the person on the street. She will be moved with compassion for those who need assistance and do whatever she can to help, while preserving the dignity and self-respect of others. An effective steward will pursue goodness and excellence in everything, knowing that she 'works for the Lord (Col 3:23). She exhibits gentleness in dealing with others, communicating, and acting in a humble way to treat people with respect, as Jesus did. The effective steward learns self-control: resisting the temptations to consume more than one needs; food, sex, alcohol; wanting more luxury, more ease, more stuff, and learning instead to let go of needing the newest, latest, and greatest. The effective steward instead get satisfaction in loving God, in giving, in engaging in healthy relationships and in living an authentic, contented, disciplined life.

That last part, self-control, hit a thread with Thomas. Self-control was what he learned, and was still putting into practice, from the Old Testament. That's why the tithe was important, it helps him practice self-control by putting first things first with what God entrusted to him to be an effective steward.

This reminded Thomas of the verse from 1 John 3:17, "If anyone has material possessions and sees his brother in need but has no pity on him, how can the love of God be in him." Thom realized that we love because he first loved us (1 John 4:20). From that love we reciprocate God's love by following his commands (2 John 1:6). That is why we discipline ourselves, why we share our possession. It is our way of showing the love God first showed us.

The truth Thom was discovering through studying his Word is God accepts us just as Jesus accepted Zacchaeus (John 8:31–37, Luke 19:1–10). God loves us and accepts us just as we are. God also loves us too much to leave us where we are, just like Zacchaeus, stuck up a tree. God has the power to change our lives. God's truth can transform us and set us free. That is what Jesus did for Zacchaeus and that is what God can do for us.

AGAPE GIVING AND ITS BLESSINGS

Thomas was at work when one of his co-workers passed him a file folder. You know the one; it has a card in it you're supposed to sign, then maybe give a small donation to buy a gift for the person you're signing the card for. It felt so forced to Thomas and wasn't pleasant. Not at all like he was learning about giving from a cheerful heart. Thom looked up the word cheerful on his smartphone and found it is translated from the Greek word agape. Thom made a connection that the giving God desires springs from a heart of love and sacrifice for others.

On his commute home, Thom thought we Christians often give sparingly and squeamishly. We give sparingly because we are afraid that we may run out money and not be able to provide for our needs. That was his struggle and the crux of how to reconcile these feelings with being a cheerful giver.

When he got home, he looked up that passage again about being a cheerful giver, this time in the King James version. It read, "God loveth a cheerful giver (2 Cor 9:7)." What Thomas learned is the Greek word for cheerful in this passage is actually the word we have derived for hilarious. God doesn't want us to just have a smirk or small grin on our face when we give; he wants us to be excited almost to point of laughter. Okay, Thom thought, but what about my fearful feelings?

As he continued his studies, Thomas realized that fear and faith often go hand in hand. By nature, when we pursue a growing faith, we increase our exposure to potential fears. It's no accident that the Bible address this condition head-on. There are a plethora of verses designed to help us let go of our fears and embrace our God-given calling to be generous stewards rather than sparingly, squeamishly, fearful owner. In Matthew 6:33, Jesus assures us that when we seek his kingdom first with our seeds, we need not fear being able to provide for our needs or being wiped out.

Something caught Thomas' eye. It was the next verse. "And God is able to make all grace abound to you, so that in all things at all times, having all that you need, you will abound in every good work (2 Cor 9:8)." Then it clicked for Thom. This is essentially saying his giving is what makes God able. Able to do what? To make all grace abound toward him. Because of Thomas' cheerful, agape, hilarious act of love through giving, he need not be sparing, squeamish or fearful. Because God makes grace, blessing, supporting all around him in all things at all times, having all that he needs. It harken back to the first disciplines he learned. Don't trust in yourself, trust in God; to let go and let God. Let God be able to make all grace abound to you.

Thom reexamined chapters eight and nine of Second Corinthians and discovered there are several blessing through the Grace of Giving. The first blessing is joy (2 Cor 8:2). Giving to meet the need of others such as pastors, missionaries, or others with needs, fills us with boundless joy. There is little that brings greater satisfaction and joy to another person than the gift of your time, abilities, or finances.

The second blessing of the Grace of Giving is an increased ability to give (2 Cor 9:7-11). God says as we faithfully give, or sow, he will increase the harvest or reap. Giving expecting to see ways in which God increase your harvest and your ability to give again.

The third blessing of the Grace of Giving is an increased attitude of thankfulness to God for his blessings (2 Cor 9:12). Paul used the word abundant in reference to thankfulness. Abundance means having so much of something that it cannot be contained, and it naturally spills out. Giving will produce an attitude of thankfulness so abundant that it cannot be contained within us. There will be a natural outpouring of praise and thanksgiving to God. The final blessing of the Grace of Giving is glory to Jesue the Christ (2 Cor 9:13-14). As you give you provide great testimony and credence to the power of God in your life. Others will take notice of your love, good spirit, and joy, and then glorify God.

Thomas reminds himself that everything belongs to God. We are simply his stewards and are to manage all that he has given us to bring him glory. God had given us his Holy Spirit, who gifts us, empowers us, and enables us for our ministry. God had given us our very lives, our time, our possessions; every resource we could possibly need, including his name and the power of that name. God had given and in more than adequate measure. We are able because God Himself has enabled us.

It is entirely a matter of whether or not we are willing, entirely a matter of whether we are willing to be faithful and obedient to this calling and this mission God has given us.

If the grace of giving is going to be evident in our lives, we must first give ourselves completely to God and then to the leadership of our church to be used in ministering according to God's will. We must first be willing to give ourselves before we will be willing to give our money as God directs. The grace of giving is giving ourselves to God to use as he chooses. The grace of giving is joyful giving. The grace of giving is a willing ministry to others.

Pray

Holy Spirit strengthen my resolve to live every day as a committed, involved disciple. Live in me and permeate my life with love. Keep me mindful of the benefits of your grace. Amen.

Stewardship

A Spirit-Filled Great Commission

THOMAS COULD FEEL HIS journey of discovering what stewardship meant was coming to a close. He would soon be moving to the next stage and begin fully living what he learned about what stewardship meant. He was almost ready to put on the Uniform of the Steward and be a partner in God's creation. There were still a few loose threads we wanted to trim before completing his pattern and sewing his vest together. He had read a lot, talked a lot with his friends and ministers about stewardship. Now we wanted to write it all down so it made better sense to him, so he could see the pattern of his uniform of the steward as a whole. He had been writing random thoughts here and there and taking notes. It was time to organize them. As he began organizing, he produced a summary of what he had learned so far:

Stewardship is more than a duty; it is a calling, a divine responsibility embedded within the Great Commission. Rooted in spiritual commitment, stewardship is not just about managing resources but embodying the character and mission of Christ. The uniform of the steward is a symbol of a life surrendered to God's service, equipped by the Holy Spirit to continue the work Christ began.

Stewardship as a Divine Mandate

From the beginning, God entrusted humanity with the care of creation, charging us to be fruitful and multiply, to subdue the earth, and to act as caretakers of his kingdom. This mandate is not only practical but spiritual, a reflection of our partnership with God in the ongoing work of redemption. The Great Commission, where Jesus commands his disciples to go into all the world, baptizing and teaching, parallels the call to stewardship.

We are stewards of the gospel, tasked with spreading its truth and living out its principles.

In this sense, stewardship becomes a spirit-filled endeavor, for we cannot accomplish the mission of God without the guidance and power of the Holy Spirit. Just as Jesus promised the Holy Spirit would empower the early church, so too does he equip modern-day stewards to carry out their divine commission.

The Spirit-Filled Nature of Stewardship

A steward in the biblical sense is more than a manager of resources; they are an administrator of God's grace, empowered by the Holy Spirit to wisely handle what God has given. This is reflected in the gifts of the Spirit, which enable believers to serve effectively, from preaching the gospel to acts of mercy and hospitality.

The parable of the talents (Matt 25:14–30) illustrates the spiritual dimension of stewardship. Each servant was given resources according to their ability, and their faithfulness in managing those resources was a measure of their devotion to the master. In the same way, believers today are entrusted with spiritual and material resources, and the Holy Spirit guides us in how to multiply these for the kingdom of God.

Stewardship as Worship and Obedience

A critical aspect of spirit-filled stewardship is that it is an act of worship. Just as offerings in the Old Testament were given as a symbol of devotion to God, so too is modern stewardship an expression of our love and obedience to the Lord. This kind of giving goes beyond the material and reaches into the very heart of what it means to be a disciple of Christ.

Spirit-filled stewardship aligns our hearts with God's purposes. As stewards, we must cultivate a posture of humility, recognizing that everything we have—our time, talents, and treasures—belongs to God. By living in accordance with his will, we demonstrate our trust in his provision and his plan.

The Role of the Holy Spirit in Stewardship

The Holy Spirit plays an essential role in shaping us as stewards. He helps us to discern God's will in how we manage our lives, guiding our decisions and actions in accordance with biblical principles. In the book of Acts, we see how the early church, filled with the Holy Spirit, practiced stewardship through generosity, sharing all they had to ensure no one was in need.

> If we are unwilling to do the ridiculous,
> then God cannot do the miraculous.

The Spirit not only leads us in generosity but also in discipline and accountability. True stewardship is more than just giving; it is about managing all of life's resources—spiritual, physical, and material—under God's guidance. The fruit of the Spirit, including self-control and faithfulness, are key to living out this responsibility.

Stewardship as a Continuation of the Great Commission

The Great Commission calls us to go, teach, and baptize, but it also calls us to be faithful stewards of the truth we carry. Stewardship, therefore, is not just about material wealth but about the gospel itself. As spirit-filled stewards, we are entrusted with the message of salvation, and we must manage this precious gift with care, ensuring that it is shared, nurtured, and multiplied in the lives of others.

This partnership with God in the mission of stewardship is a privilege and a responsibility. We are not just caretakers of the earth or our resources, but of the spiritual truths that can transform lives. Through the power of the Holy Spirit, we are equipped to fulfill this high calling, living as faithful stewards until Christ returns.

Thomas concluded his summary by writing:

Stewardship as a great commission is not just about managing what God has given us, but about fulfilling his divine purpose through the power of the Holy Spirit. It is a calling to live a life of service, to multiply the gifts and resources God has entrusted to us, and to spread the gospel with faithfulness and diligence. As stewards, we partner with God in the ongoing work of redemption, clothed in the uniform of faithful service, empowered by the Spirit, and committed to the mission of Christ.

Let us, therefore, embrace stewardship not as a burden but as a spirit-filled commission, a way of life that glorifies God and advances his kingdom.

MATERIALISM

Thomas was at Wednesday night bible study and the associate pastor began with:

> Watch out! Be on your guard against all kinds of greed; a man's life does not consist in the abundance of his possessions (Luke 12:13–15).

She went on to say, Webster's Dictionary defines materialism as the tendency to be more concerned with material things than spiritual values. Materialism gets even the best of us. The riches of Christ's kingdom are far greater than anything on earth. Just read Colossians 3:4 to see what I mean. It's easy for us to become preoccupied with money and the material things of this world. We tend to think that we have earned them by the sweat of our brow or the cleverness of our thinking, forgetting that everything we have comes from God. In truth, we are merely stewards, or custodians, of what he chooses to give us.

Second Corinthians 5:10 and Romans 14:10 tells us that Christians will one day stand at the judgment seat of Christ, where we will give an account of the works we have done. We will be called to explain what we have done with our lives, our gifts and abilities, and our monies and possessions. Revelation 20:11–15 shows us the consequences of not being a steward as it tells us of God's judgment of those who remain dead in their trespasses and sins because they rejected life. They refused to believe in Jesus and receive him as their Lord and their God, to have him reign over them. Even in the lake of fire there will be degrees of punishment according to a person's deeds. God is just. Always. With all people.

With that associate pastor Sarah opened up the discussion to the group to share what they have learned from these sobering truths. And their discussion took up their remaining time together.

On the drive home Thomas was debating with himself whether something was a want or need; especially in light of tonight's bible study discussion. Then he realized such a debate is a lose-lose deal because the messages of consumption clobber us from every angle. He thought what he has right now is enough. If he is faithful in trivial things, he will be entrusted with more. Just like at work, as he showed he could handle more responsibility, more was given to him. He was learning to live on the amount of money he has now and enjoy the setting in which he found himself, which was bringing him contentment. And he was learning the secret to wealth: how to manage his finances when he had very little trained him to better manage his finances when he has more. He thought to himself, "I do have enough right now. My needs are met." He was learning to use that enough in such a way that it is moving him into financial confidence and freedom.

The realization Thom came to is Jesus is not saying that we cannot have things. He is saying to watch out for thinking we own our possessions. We may wake up someday to find the possessions own us. Riches and possessions are certainly available to us without "the blessings of the Lord," he pondered. Just look around you. However, riches and possessions do not impress God, because he knew they are his anyway, and they definitely do not usher the presence of God into your life. Conversely, Thom surmised, "the blessing of the Lord" do encompass all riches, both spiritual and natural. Revelation 2:23 confirms this truth, "I am he who searches hearts and minds, and I will repay each of you according to your deeds."

As Thomas was going through his nightly routine getting ready for bed, he was reasoning what does this materialism mean for stewardship? As he mulled over this question the answer, he derived is it means that we must acknowledge that the sinful desires and inclinations that come from deep within us keep us from doing what we are called to do. We cannot always discern what they are, where they lurk and how they have disguised themselves. But scripture suggests a couple: the lust of the eyes and pride in possessions (1 John 2:16). To discern these negatives, a steward must allow God to search a person's heart and mind, "for the word of God is living and active. Sharper than any double-edged sword, it penetrates even to dividing soul and spirit, joints and marrow; it judges the thoughts and attitudes of the heart (Hebrews 4:12)." It is also a matter of study and discernment in recognizing the subtle and not-so-subtle influences of the world and its attitudes towards service, spiritually, money, possessions, time, environment and all types of relationships. We can steward our hearts by being mindful of what we absorb through our senses, not only keeping out the bad influences but taking in the good, just like Philippians 4:8 tells us.

For his evening prayer, Thomas read Ephesians 2:8–10, "For we are God's workmanship, created in Christ Jesus to do good works, which God prepared in advance for us to do." he then drifted off to sleep.

MONEY, WHAT A TOOL

Thomas was at work laboring on setting up one of the industrial cutting machines for a new pattern his company was introducing. This lead him to a stream of consciousness about tools, money, and how a good steward views cash. Money, in the Christian worldview, is not an end in itself but a tool. Like any tool, it has the power to build or destroy, depending on how it is used. Thom realized the Bible offers profound insights into the purpose and role of money in our lives, urging believers to handle it with wisdom and caution. We are reminded that while money can serve God's purposes, it can also lead to spiritual ruin when improperly prioritized.

Thomas recalled his Old Testament foundations of a biblical perspective on money begins with recognizing God as the sovereign Creator and Lord over all things. In Acts 17:22-31, Paul, speaking to the Athenians, declares, "The God who made the world and everything in it is the Lord of heaven and earth." God is not dependent on anything we offer, including our money. Instead, everything we possess is a gift from him, and we are merely stewards of his creation.

This understanding shifts our view of money. It is not ours to hoard or misuse, but rather a resource entrusted to us by God. As stewards, our role is to manage it in a way that honors him and aligns with his purposes. Thom knows the temptation to idolize wealth is strong, but as Paul warns in 1 Timothy 6:10, "For the love of money is a root of all kinds of evil. Some people, eager for money, have wandered from the faith and pierced themselves with many griefs."

Paul's words in 1 Timothy 6:6-11 provide a crucial framework for understanding the dangers of placing money above God. He explains that "godliness with contentment is great gain," and that we brought nothing into this world, and we can take nothing out. Verses 7-9 emphasize the fleeting nature of material wealth: "For we brought nothing into the world, and we can take nothing out of it. But if we have food and clothing, we will be content with that. Those who want to get rich fall into temptation and a trap and into many foolish and harmful desires that plunge people into ruin and destruction.

The pursuit of wealth, when it becomes the ultimate goal, leads to spiritual bankruptcy. This scripture highlights the contrast between godliness and the desire for wealth, cautioning believers that money itself is not evil, but the love of it is dangerous. It can cause individuals to wander from the faith, lured by the promises of material security, only to find themselves lost and burdened with grief.

Just then Thomas felt a sharp pain on his fingers. He grasped he pinched them with channel locks he was using to set up the machinery. So much for paying attention to what he was doing. He would pick up his thoughts about money being a tool later, after work. For now, he would do most of his concentrating on his job.

Later that evening, Thom was noticing his New Testament lessons and read how Jesus makes it clear in Matthew 6:24 that "No one can serve two masters. Either you will hate the one and love the other, or you will be devoted to the one and despise the other. You cannot serve both God and money." This verse is pivotal in understanding the Christian approach to wealth. Serving money leads to a divided heart, pulling us away from our true calling to serve God with undivided devotion. Like, not paying attention at work and pinching yourself with the tools you're using.

Thom was contemplating, does this mean we should abandon money or ignore its role in our lives? No, he considered. Instead, we must conquer it—putting it in its proper place, recognizing it as a tool to accomplish God's work. The only way to serve God effectively is through proper stewardship of money, not by making it our master but by mastering it. We are called to catch up with God's plan for our lives by aligning our financial practices with his will.

To use money as a tool for God's kingdom, we must conquer our desire for wealth and learn to manage it wisely. This is the essence of biblical financial stewardship. God's resources are to be multiplied and used to advance his kingdom, not squandered or idolized. Just as Jesus taught in the parable of the talents (Matthew 25:14–30), we are to invest what he has given us wisely, ensuring that we are faithful stewards.

The apostle Paul, in 1 Timothy 6:17–18, concludes with a message to those who are wealthy: "Command those who are rich in this present world not to be arrogant nor to put their hope in wealth, which is so uncertain, but to put their hope in God, who richly provides us with everything for our enjoyment. Command them to do good, to be rich in good deeds, and to be generous and willing to share."

This final charge is a reminder that the true purpose of wealth is not personal comfort or status, but generosity. Those who have been blessed with financial resources are called to use them for good—to support the needs of others and further the work of God's kingdom.

Thomas came to the conclusion that money, while a powerful tool, must be placed under the lordship of Christ. It can either be a resource for advancing God's purposes or a snare leading us away from him. By recognizing that all we have comes from God and is to be used for his glory, we are able to put money in its proper place. When we conquer our desire for wealth and serve God with all we have, we align ourselves with his greater plan for our lives, experiencing the true joy and freedom that come from godly stewardship.

That night Thomas prayed:

> Heavenly Father,
> You are the Creator and Lord of all things. Everything in this world belongs to You, including the money and resources

we possess. I humbly acknowledge that You have entrusted me with these gifts, not for my own gain, but to be a faithful steward of Your kingdom. Lord, help me to see money not as a master, but as a tool—one that can be used to serve You and bring glory to Your name.

Forgive me for the times when I have allowed the love of money to distract me from my true calling. I confess that I have sometimes sought security in wealth rather than in You, and in doing so, I have wandered from the path of righteousness. Guard my heart, Lord, and teach me to find contentment in Your provision, knowing that I brought nothing into this world and can take nothing out of it.

Help me to conquer the temptation to serve money. Strengthen me to put it in its proper place, using it wisely to fulfill Your purposes. May I always seek first Your kingdom and righteousness, trusting that You will provide for my every need.

Guide me, Lord, as I seek to be generous, willing to share the blessings You have given me with others. May my financial decisions reflect a heart that is fully devoted to You. Give me wisdom to manage what You have placed in my care, and may I be a faithful steward of both small and great resources.

Thank You, Father, for being my Provider. Help me to put my hope not in wealth, but in You, who richly provides for my enjoyment. May I always seek to honor You in all that I do, knowing that true riches are found in a life lived for Your glory.

In Jesus' name, Amen.

KINGDOMS COME

What Thomas was discovering is the New Testament goes into great detail about two kingdoms, the Kingdom of God and the Kingdom of Heaven. He knew it is important that we understand what the Lord means by each kingdom. The Kingdom of God is the supernatural life we were created to enjoy here and now, on earth, by living in and through the Holy Spirit. As Romans 14:17-18 states:

> For the kingdom of God is not a matter of eating and drinking, but of righteousness, peace and joy in the Holy Spirit, because anyone who serves Christ in this way is pleasing to God and approved by men.

When Christ returned to Heaven, he sent the Holy Spirit to help us boldly abide in the Kingdom of God during our time on earth. The believer's life on earth is meant to glorify God, and should be recognized by its abundant joy, peace, and righteousness. Christ, through the work of the Holy Spirit, has arranged a safe harbor for us here on earth. That safe harbor is the Kingdom of God. It is in the Holy Spirit that we will find a peace beyond understanding, regardless of our circumstances. But it is hard for us to remain in the Kingdom of God and walk in the Spirit, because Satan uses temptations and deception to constantly war against our flesh, our souls, and our minds. As Thom found in Galatians 5:19–21:

> The acts of the sinful nature are obvious: sexual immorality, impurity and debauchery; idolatry and witchcraft; hatred, discord, jealousy, fits of rage, selfish ambition, dissensions, faction and envy; drunkenness, orgies, and the like. I warn you, as I did before, that those who like this will not inherit the Kingdom of God.

Sadly, one of Satan's most powerful tools is to distract us from God's perfect will for our lives by luring us with the false promises of wealth.

The first destruction, the deceitfulness of wealth, takes place here on earth, in the kingdom of God. Both the believer and the unsaved can fall victim to it. It is the third seed described by Jesus in his parable of the Sower:

> The one who received the seed that fell among the thorns is the man who hears the word, but the worries of this life and the deceitfulness of wealth choke it, making it unfruitful (Matt 13:22).

The second destruction brought about by deception of wealth is seldom discussed Thomas thought, but even more tragic. This deception involves the eternal Kingdom of Heaven. The second deception of wealth is the most devastating because the loss is eternal. Through his studies, Thom comprehended it is when we stand before the Lord and he reveals the eternal rewards that we have lost because we chose to chase after the temporal. From his New Testament lesson Thomas grasped scripture is so clear on this point: God has an eternal purpose for our life that is outside the calendar of our years on earth. Thomas remembers Ephesians 2:10, "For we are . . . created in Christ Jesus to do good works, which God prepared in advance for us to do." And 1 John 2:17, "The world and its desires pass away, but the man who does the will of God lives forever."

Continuing his exploration of the two kingdoms, Thom realized, the 25th chapter of Matthew's gospel begins with nine incredibly significant words: "At that time the Kingdom of Heaven is like . . . " and then continues with the stories, one of which is this story of the man and servants, or more accurately, the story of how it is between us and the only true living God. For Thom this tied back to Matthew 6:33, "Seek first his kingdom and his righteousness and all these things will be given to you as well." Which related back to what we learned about Godly freedom.

Godly Freedom; a supernatural release that you receive when you have purpose in your heart to serve God instead of money. It is at this point, when you have chosen to no longer worry about tomorrow, that the supernatural and the miraculous become commonplace in your life.

It made sense to Thomas. He was recalling what he learned about money. It is neither evil nor good. It is what you do with it that colors it with moral relativity. Money simply makes you more of what you already were before you had it. If you were a giver before you had money, you will still be generous once you have wealth. Money shows your values and preferences. It you want to know who you really are, all you need to do is look at your spending habits. What you do with your money shows you what you love and value. Is it the Kingdom of God, while here on earth. Or the temptations of Satan.

If we our managing our wealth according to the Kingdom of God, it affects our relationship with what we own that goes beyond the rules and regulations of the natural world. We grasp that the pursuit of prosperity is as much a spiritual battle as it is a natural one. In the book of Ephesians Thomas read about this battle:

> For our struggle is not against flesh and blood, but against the rulers, against the authorities, against the powers of this dark world and against the spiritual forces of evil in the heavenly realms (Eph 6:12).

Thom was seeing a pattern. He was a tailor, after all. Jesus frequently uses money to describe the meaning, characteristics, and dynamics of the Kingdom of God. Thomas saw it as God's pattern for financial abundance. In Thom's mind the pattern goes something like this:

Faith + Good Stewardship + Giving = Abundance.

What Thomas was deciphering was that by being good stewards with what God has given us while living in the Kingdom of God, we are building up our true wealth in the Kingdom of Heaven.

OUR MISSION—GIVEN

The big pattern Thomas was picturing from his New Testament lessons was investing in Great Commission causes in this life prepares us for our role in eternity. He recognized accumulating and holding wealth on earth doesn't improve your status in heaven. At least not according to the scriptures he read. However, the distribution of his earthly wealth to advance God's kingdom will. That's the promise he wasn't missing. It's also the test that God uses to help us understand what we have placed first in our lives. From what Thom had learned so far, how we spend our money is an exact reflection of our heart condition. No faithful steward chooses what is important to his master or overrides his master's expressed interests.

Thom reread the passages about the Great Commission (Matt 28:16–20, Mark 16:14–20, Luke 24: 45–53, John 20:19–23, and Acts 1:8). The verse that stuck with him the most was Matthew 28:20, "and teaching them to obey everything I have commanded you. And surely, I am with you always, to the very end of the age." That's exactly what he was doing; learning, being taught, to obey his commands. To be a good steward who has a grateful and disciplined response of his whole person to continue the work Christ began. To dress himself for a life of faithful service as a partner in God's creation. And when that faithful service was proving difficult, Jesus would be there with him-to the very end of the age.

An insight swept over Thomas, that all of his disciplining from the Old Testament and learning from the New Testament he was doing for himself to learn what are the quality materials that make up stewardship didn't stop once he found his answers. It didn't stop once he had those quality materials that he could craft a pattern that could be sewn together into a uniform, a uniform he could wear. A uniform that had embroidered into it both spiritual and financial prosperity. A uniform that let him be a faithful servant to God. A uniform that let him focus on higher things. Once you put on a Uniform of the Steward it also includes a responsibility. Part of focusing on higher things includes teaching others "to obey everything I have commended you." That sent chills through Thomas' body. What began as self-help for himself, so he could feel less anxious about his financial worries, led him to fathom he was now part of the Great Commission and had an obligation to teach others what he had learned.

A cunning smile came across his face when Thom recognized what God was doing in his life. Anytime God calls, God equips. Anytime God sends, God empowers. Anytime God gives a task, a mission, or a responsibility, God give every resource needed to carry it out. God had given Thomas every resource he needed to carry out the responsibility and mission of putting on the Uniform of the Steward. Thom recalled what Moses told the Israelite's, "Remember the Lord your God, for it is he who give you the ability to produce wealth (Dt 8:18)." Wealth that Thomas will use to build the Kingdom of God. Which reminded him of what the apostle Paul said, "Whatever you do, do it all for the glory of God (1 Cor 10:31)."

> Don't let your worries get the best of you.
> Remember, Moses started out as a basket case.

It seemed like an impossible task. Learning about stewardship was easy, compared to teaching others about it. Thom didn't feel at all confident about this newly discovered mission God was assigning to him. Yes, he knew God would provide, Jesus would be there for him, the Holy spirit would help him. Still, it didn't alleviate his confidence obstacle. Then he recalled the apostle Peter had an impossible task—walking on water—yet he accomplished it (Matt 14:22-31). Thomas contemplated how Peter did it. In studying this passage Thom found Peter took two steps, literally and figuratively. First, he took a risk. The disciples saw Jesus walking toward them in the storm. After Jesus declared that he was not a ghost, Peter took two risks by 1: asking Jesus to call him out onto the water, and 2: actually stepping out on the water with Jesus. The second step Peter took was trust Jesus to hold him up. Peter got out of the boat and walked on the water towards Jesus. He was focusing on Jesus after he took the risk to go out on the water, and it worked. But it also says that on his way to Jesus, he looked at the storm and began to doubt, which caused him to sink. This caused him to cry out to Jesus to save him. Peter had forgotten totally what he was doing before he began to sink. He lost his focus and was not able to regain it when the turmoil overwhelmed him. Jesus was still there to save the day. The lesson Thomas learned, and would teach others, is let's be found in faith, not in doubt. When he had doubts, he would have faith the Holy Spirit would show him the way.

Wading on the Waters

Thomas found that the way God works is quirky. Which was what was happening right now. He was at Bible Study and the group was discussing the upcoming Layperson Sunday. It was a Sunday, usually a fifth Sunday of a month, were the lay people of the church would lead the entire service. Associate Pastor Sarah was suggesting Thomas do the sermon about his stewardship journey. Of course, the rest of the group wholeheartedly endorsed the suggestion. Thomas' suspicion was because none of them wanted to be volunteered for the task.

Thom reluctantly agreed to give the sermon. He figured this was God's quirky way of propelling him into the next stage of his stewardship journey, to begin "teaching them."

That Friday night, Thomas sat down to write his first ever sermon. He prayed for Jesus to be there with him and the Holy Spirit to inspire him. A few hours later, with some revisions, spell checks, and reference confirmations, he finished. That Sunday this is what he preached:

"There is a story about a mother and son who lived in a forest. One day when they were out a tornado surprised them. The mother clung to a tree and tried to hold her son. But the swirling winds carried him into the sky. He was gone.

The woman began to weep and pray, "Please, O Lord, bring back my boy! He's all I have. I'd do anything not to lose him. If you'll bring him back, I'll serve you all my days." Suddenly the boy toppled from the sky, right at her feet; a bit mussed up, but unharmed.

His mother joyfully brushed him off. Then she stopped for a moment, looked to the sky, and said, "He had a hat, Lord."

"This story is a good illustration of our attitude toward the money and possessions God has given us. Even when God blesses us greatly, we still want a little more.

When it comes to finances, many of God's people live in a constant state of dissatisfaction with what they have. The reason is that we are all born as sinners, and all sinners are natural materialist. The dictionary defines materialism as the theory or doctrine that physical well-being and possessions constitute the greatest good and highest value in life. If you are a Christian, you would deny that you believe in materialism. But many Christians, who are not materialists in theory, are materialist in practice. You know you are practicing materialist if there is a certain amount of money you think you must accumulate, or something you believe you must buy before you can be happy. What is it you are waiting to have before you will be satisfied? Mini-van, newer, house, new bedroom furniture, new truck, or vacation to Disney World?"

"Financial discontent ruins marriages, causes parents to neglect their children, rob people of joy, and cause the work of God to go without adequate financial support around the world."

How can we find financial contentment? The answer is found in God's Word. In Philippians 4:10–14. Turn with me to this scripture and let's read it together:

'I rejoice greatly in the Lord that at last you have renewed your concern for me. Indeed, you have been concerned, but you had no opportunity to show it. I am not saying this because I am in need, for I have learned to be content whatever the circumstances. I know what it is to be in need, and I know what it is to have plenty. I have learned the secret of being content in any and every situation, whether well fed or hungry, whether living in plenty or in want. I can do everything through him who gives me strength.

Yet it was good for you to share in my troubles.'

"The apostle Paul teaches us six principles of financial contentment. The first principles provides us with a definition. Financial contentment is the ability to be satisfied in plenty or poverty (Philippians 4:10-12). The Philippians had sent a financial gift with Epaphroditus and Paul rejoices because they had revived their concern for his welfare while in prison. Paul says they had always been concerned but had laced opportunity to express their concern practically. 'Lacked opportunity' probably means either they lacked money, as they were a very poor church, or they lacked a messenger; no one may have been able to make the trip with the gift. But now at last Epaphroditus had come with their gift and Paul was very pleased."

"In verses 11 and 12 Paul says he has learned to be content in plenty or poverty. In Greek, content is autarkes, which means self-sufficient, emotionally independent of changing financial circumstances. The Greek Stoic philosophers in the ancient world used this Greek word to describe a person who had the inner strength to face whatever happen to them, good or bad, with neither joy nor sorrow. The Stoics considered the achieving of 'self-sufficiency' to be the ultimate goal in life. When Paul said he was content, he used this word to mean he was not dependent on money for satisfaction in life.

"I know this is not true for most people. Most of us are dependent on a good bank account and an upwardly progressing income and standard of living for our happiness. We believe the bumper sticker that says, 'The one who dies with the most toys wins.' According to God's word financial contentment is the ability to be satisfied in plenty or poverty."

"The second principle of financial contentment is that financial contentment is possible (Philippians 4:11-12). The apostle Paul testified truthfully that he was financially content in both plenty and poverty. Paul's appreciation for their gift was not expressed out of a sense of need of dissatisfaction with his circumstance. Remember, he was content in plenty and poverty. He was content in plenty, prosperity, being filled, having abundance. Paul was happy and satisfied when he had plenty of financial resources and when his stomach was full."

"That wasn't too difficult. But he was also content in poverty, humble means, going hungry, suffering need. Paul writes about his contentment with poverty while on house arrest in Rome. By this time he has been in prison about four years, two years in Caesarea and two in Rome. This is hard for Paul. He is an activist. He is a religious entrepreneur. He had expressed a strong desire to travel to Spain as a pioneer missionary. He is goal driven. Yet God has confirmed him in prison for the last four years of his life. In Rome he is chained twenty-four hours a day to a Roman guard. He has no privacy day or night. And he is barely surviving financially. Yet he claims he is content, satisfied and joyful." Elsewhere in Philippians he says, 'Finally, my brethren, rejoice in the Lord (Philippians 3:1). Rejoice in the Lord always; again I will say, rejoice (Philippians 4:4). We know it is possible to be financially content because Paul was. It is possible for you and me to be satisfied with less than we would like to have. It is possible for us to be content with old clothes, a small house, a beat-up car, or no money to eat out."

"The third principle of financial contentment is that financial contentment is a secret to be learned (Philippians 4:11–12). Twice Paul speaks of learning to be content. Both in verse 11 and verse 12, I have learned to be content.' 'I have learned the secret of being filled and going hungry.' he uses two different Greek words for learned. In verse 11 it is learn through experience. In verse 12 it is learn a secret not known to everybody. Literally, I have been initiated into a secret. In the Greek perfect tense it would be I have been initiated into a secret which I have permanently mastered. Paul's financial contentment was not something he got automatically at his conversion on the road to Damascus. He had to learn to be content. God took him through many difficult experiences of plenty and poverty before he had finally permanently learned to be financially satisfied in any circumstance. "

"We too will have to learn to be content. Contentment must be learned because it is not natural. As sinners we are naturally born discontent with our financial state. You see this in kids. After they open a shameful amount of presents on Christmas day, they ask, 'Is this all there is?' We always want more. We always think we would be happy if we could make just a little more money. Somebody once asked the wealth Joh D. Rockefeller, 'How much does it take to satisfy a man?' Rockefeller answered, 'A bit more than he has.' God teaches us by experience to be content with plenty or poverty."

"I've seen God do this in my life. There have been times like today when I have an abundance of money and possessions, I live in a nice house in a nice neighborhood. I drive a nice car. I work at a place that has central air conditioning. And I make a good wage. But there was a time when I worked in a hot and dirty sweat shop factory. I lived in a tiny, ugly, dirty shack in somebody's backyard. And I wasn't even making minimum wage. I still have more to learn, but God has used these varied circumstance in my life to teach me to be equally satisfied with plenty or poverty."

"God is using the difficulties of your financial life experiences to teach you several lessons that produce financial contentment. Lessons that produce financial contentment are:

"Money cannot satisfy. 'He who loves money will not be satisfied with money, nor he who loves abundance with its income. This too is vanity (Ecclesiastes 5:10)." Money will buy a bed but not sleep; books but not brains; food but not appetite; finery bit not beauty; religion but not salvation; a passport to everywhere but heaven."

"Love of money will produce misery. 'But godliness actually is a means of great gain, when accompanied by contentment. For we have brought nothing into the world, so we cannot take anything out of it either. And if we have food and covering, with these we shall be content. But those who want to get rich fall into temptation and a snare and many foolish and harmful desires which plunge men into ruin and destruction. For the love of money is a root of all sorts of evil, and some by longing for it have wandered away from the faith and pierced themselves with many a pang (1Tim 6:6–10).'"

"Money provides a false sense of security. 'Instruct those who are rich in this present world not to be conceited or to fix their hope on the uncertainty of riches, but on God, who richly supplies us with all things to enjoy (1Tim 6:17).'"

"God can be trusted to meet all your needs for money. Let your character be free from the love of money, being content with what you have; for he Himself has said, "I will never desert you, nor will I ever forsake you." So that we confidently say, "The Lord is my helper, I will not be afraid. What shall man do to me (Hebrews 13:5–6)?"

"C.S. Lewis wrote, 'He who has God and everything has no more than he who has God alone.' God alone is the source of everything. You have no more real security for the future with $10,000 in a saving account than if you have $10 in your pocket. God Himself has promised to never desert or forsake you. Knowing that God has promised and can be trusted to meet all your monetary needs will enable you to be satisfied with whatever you have."

"The forth principle of financial contentment is that a grateful spirit accompanies financial contentment (Philippians 4:10–14). Even though Paul was in prison and in poverty, he was grateful for what the Philippians sent him as is witnessed in verse 10, 'I rejoiced greatly. . .' and in verse 14, 'You have done well. . .' as in you did a noble, a beautiful thing in sending me a gift. Paul says thanks. He doesn't expect them to know he is grateful or to assume he is thankful. Instead he made doubly sure they know how much he appreciated their financial gift. Paul's satisfaction with poverty made him deeply grateful for anything he received."

"You see, a discontented person is usually an ungrateful person. The discontented person is filled with self-pity because he doesn't have more. And she really believes they deserve to have more. So they find it difficult to be truly grateful when someone gives them something. I have a Chirstian friend at another parish who is a dentist. She gives pastors free dental care, and their families receive a fifty percent discount. She has indicated to me on more than one occasion over the years as I have thanked her for her generosity, that some pastors she helps do not even say thank you. They act as if they are owed this benefit because they have sacrificed a more lucrative career to go into the ministry. This is totally uncoordinated with the apostle Paul. It is the result of financial discontentment."

"Somebody has said, 'The things we take for granted are dreams to many people.' When we remember that we in America are richer than 95 percent of the world's population, it will help us be more content and more grateful. Are you a grateful person? Do you freely express thanks when someone gives you a gift or in any way expresses a desire to help you financially? Do you expect people to assume you are thankful? Or do you act as if you had it coming?"

"The fifth principle of financial contentment is that God requires financial contentment (Philippians 4:11–12, Hebrews 13:5). Paul's example of contentment has the force of a command. He was content in plenty and poverty. God expects you and me to me content as well. And we have seen that God explicitly commands us to be financially content in Hebrews 13:5. It is God's will that you and I be completely satisfied with him and with life whether we are rich or poor. The Stoics could only achieve a counterfeit version of contentment by denying their emotions and desires. They had a survivor mentally which achieved inner peace by killing all longings and all feelings so as to never feel again. This is as good as men get in our own strength. But God commands us to have a joyful satisfaction that is independent of our financial circumstances. That is humanly impossible. How can we ever get to a point where we are independent of money for happiness?"

"That leads us to our sixth principle of financial contentment, which answers this question. Financial contentment is achieved by Christ's power (Philippians 4:13). Paul didn't learn contentment by his superior intellect or will power. He achieved contentment by the power of Christ. He literally said in the Greek, 'I am strong for all things through him who continually infuses power into me.' Paul said, 'The spiritual strength to be satisfied in plenty or poverty comes from Christ who continually strengthens me.' If you want to be financially content, you will find the power in Christ alone. Jesus Christ lives in every believer. Jesus Himself lived a life of poverty with total contentment. He wants to impart to you his divine power to be content no matter what your financial circumstances." "If you would like Christ to give you his financial contentment this morning, here's all you need to: confess you sin of discontent, surrender to Christ's will for you financially, ask him in faith for his power to be content with the money and possessions he has given you."

"Pray with me. Dear Lord Jesus Christ, I confess that have sinned against you by my discontent with the money and possessions you have given to me. I now surrender to your will for me, whether it means financial plenty or poverty. By faith I ask you to empower me so that I can be satisfied with my financial condition. In Your name, Amen."

After Sunday's sermon, Thomas felt confident that he now had the quality material, the cloth, to lay his pattern against. The threads of the cloth are Prudence, Prosperity & Knowledge; and the strands that compromise these threads are careful forethought and planning, godly stewardship, and a willingness to follow instructions. He had a pattern, a Uniform of the Steward, a uniform that let him be a faithful servant to God. A uniform that let him focus on higher things and that would fit all the pieces together for him about stewardship. That pattern would be a vest because of its versatility. The first piece of the pattern, the lining, is his definition of what stewardship is:

> Stewardship is the grateful, disciplined response of the whole person continuing the work Christ began. It is dressing ourselves for a life of faithful service as partners in God's creation.

He had other pieces; a back, a left front side, a right front side, and a pocket. He knew the back piece of the pattern is God having our back by giving us his word, found in the Bible, of how to be a good steward.

The front left side of the pattern were the lessons he learned from the Old Testament, to be disciplined. The front right side were lessons he learned from the New Testament, the lessons of love. And a pocket on the front of the vest; to remind him that the left hand should not know what the right hand is doing about his offerings. And to remember to give back a small portion, a tithe, to God to show his discipleship to be his steward.

That next weekend Thomas was at work laying out the pattern, cutting the cloth, and sewing his vest, his Uniform of the Steward, together. As he was doing this, he reminisced about his journey and all that he had learned was still learning. He understood we tend to hoard our money and think that it is ours. A good steward has the reverse idea. Money is not ours; it is his. Because it is his, a steward, thinking in love, uses money to do his master's will and fulfill his kingdom. He thought God gave us three gifts, faith, hope and love. The greatest of these is love. He remembered his mom once told him that love is the gift that the more you give, the more you have to give. And you receive back more abundantly than you first gave.

That was what Thomas was going to do. He said to himself, "As a steward I'm going to treat money like love, the better I handle it the more abundantly others will be blessed, and it will come back to me in the Kingdom of Heaven."

Thomas walked out the door of work to head home wearing his new vest. He felt different, like he was wearing a new uniform and ready to walk on water.

Pray

Thank you, Lord, for the gifts of Jesus Christ and of the Holy Spirit, who enables me to be a steward of all you have entrusted to me. Amen.

Epilogue

IN THE EPILOGUE OF Thomas' stewardship journey, he finally embraces the essence of being a faithful steward of God's creation. After navigating various challenges and exploring the meaning of stewardship through the lessons learned from his family, his spiritual journey, and his growing understanding of financial responsibility, Thomas reaches a point of realization: stewardship is not just about managing material resources, but also about cultivating spiritual wealth and living a life of gratitude, discipline, and service.

Thomas recognizes that he is not the owner of the gifts and opportunities he has been given, but rather a caretaker, entrusted by God to manage them wisely. Throughout his journey, Thomas learns to trust God's provision and acknowledges that true prosperity comes from aligning his actions with God's purpose, rather than chasing worldly wealth. His experiences, from learning to give generously to balancing his resources, teach him that God's blessings flow when he is obedient, disciplined, and humble.

In the end, Thomas understands that wearing the "Uniform of the Steward" is not about outward appearances, but about embodying the principles of stewardship in every aspect of life. His journey concludes with a deepened faith and a commitment to live as a steward of God's grace, always ready to give back from the abundance he receives. His story becomes an example of how embracing stewardship transforms not only financial life but also spiritual and communal well-being, as he continues to serve as a partner with God in his creation.

Lord Jesus

My heartfelt desire is that this book has moved you toward a closer relationship with the Lord. If you do not know Jesus as your personal Lord and Savior, please pray this prayer:

> Lord Jesus, I am a sinner in need of a Savior. I believe that You are the Son of God and that You died on the cross, a living sacrifice for my sins. I surrender my life to You. Please forgive me for my sins and create in me a new heart that desires to serve You all the days of my life. I accept You as my Lord and Savior. Amen.

Bibliography

BIBLICAL REFERENCES

The Holy Bible, New International Version. Copyright © 1973, 1978, 1984 by International Bible Society. Used by permission of Zondervan. All rights reserved.
The Holy Bible, New Revised Standard Version. Copyright © 1989 by the Division of Christian Education of the National Council of Churches of Christ in the U.S.A. Used by permission. All rights reserved.
The Living Bible. Copyright © 1971 by Tyndale House Publishers. All rights reserved.
The New Jerusalem Bible. Copyright © 1999 by Doubleday, a division of Random House Inc., and Darton, Longman & Todd, Ltd. All rights reserved.
The New English Bible. Copyright © 1961, 1970, 1972 by the Delegates of the Oxford University Press and the Syndics of the Cambridge University Press. All rights reserved.

ADDITIONAL SOURCES REFERENCED IN TEXT

Chrysostom, John. *Sermons on Christian Living and Stewardship*. Translated by Catharine P. Roth. St Vladimer's Seminary, 1981.
Goins, Cliff. *Stop Digging: Biblical Principles of Financial Stewardship*. The Adelphos, 2003.
Perkins, William. *Christian Wealth and Responsibility*. Independently Published, 1580.
Wesley, John. *Sermons on Christian Stewardship*. Edited by Thomas Jackson. Christian Classics Ethereal Library, 1872.

www.ingramcontent.com/pod-product-compliance
Lightning Source LLC
Chambersburg PA
CBHW060030180426
43196CB00044B/2283